GOTHIC GEOCULTURE

GLOBAL LATIN/O AMERICAS

Frederick Luis Aldama and Lourdes Torres, Series Editors

GOTHIC GEOCULTURE

NINETEENTH-CENTURY
REPRESENTATIONS OF CUBA IN
THE TRANSAMERICAN IMAGINARY

IVONNE M. GARCÍA

THE OHIO STATE UNIVERSITY PRESS
COLUMBUS

Copyright © 2019 by The Ohio State University.
All rights reserved.

Library of Congress Cataloging-in-Publication Data
Names: García, Ivonne M., author.
Title: Gothic geoculture : nineteenth-century representations of Cuba in the transamerican imaginary / Ivonne M. García.
Other titles: Global Latin/o Americas.
Description: Columbus : The Ohio State University Press, [2019] | Series: Global Latin/o Americas | Includes bibliographical references and index.
Identifiers: LCCN 2018050728 | ISBN 9780814213957 (cloth ; alk. paper) | ISBN 0814213952 (cloth ; alk. paper)
Subjects: LCSH: Literature and society—Cuba—History—19th century. | Cuba—History—1810–1899. | Gothic revival (Literature)—History and criticism. | Corruption—Cuba.
Classification: LCC F1758 .G37 2019 | DDC 972.91/05—dc23
LC record available at https://lccn.loc.gov/2018050728

Cover image: "Liminal Transposition" by Janae A. Peters
Cover design by Angela Moody
Text design by Juliet Williams
Type set in Adobe Minion Pro

A papi y mami

CONTENTS

Acknowledgments		ix
INTRODUCTION	Gothic Geocultures in the Transamerican Imaginary	1
CHAPTER 1	Corruptive Gothicscapes: William Cullen Bryant's *Letters of a Traveller* and Nathaniel Parker Willis's *Health Trip to the Tropics*	21
CHAPTER 2	Gothicized Souths: Martin R. Delany's *Blake, or the Huts of America* and Louisa May Alcott's "Pauline's Passion and Punishment"	43
CHAPTER 3	Transgressive Hauntings: Sophia Peabody's *Cuba Journal* and Mary Peabody Mann's *Juanita: A Romance of Real Life in Cuba Fifty Years Ago*	67
CHAPTER 4	Gothic Emplotments: Cirilo Villaverde's *Cecilia Valdés* and *The Story of Evangelina Cisneros, Told by Herself*	93
CHAPTER 5	"Inside the Monster": José Martí's Decolonial Transamericanity	121
CONCLUSION	Decolonizing the Gothic	143
Bibliography		151
Index		165

ACKNOWLEDGMENTS

THEY SAY it takes a village to raise a child. Well, it has definitely taken pretty much a *pueblo* to get this manuscript to where it needed to be.

My father, who did not live to see this publication, believed one day I would publish a book, and taught me to love ghost and monster stories, preparing me for my work on the gothic. My mother, a renowned historian in her own right, showed me early in life how a woman could have intellectual ambition.

Chad Allen and Susan Williams helped model for me what it means to pursue excellence through their outstanding scholarship, citizenship, and teaching. Chad introduced me to postcolonial and postnationalist theories, and Susan introduced me to Sophia Peabody and to the *Cuba Journal*. Frederick Aldama's support for this project has also been much appreciated.

Kenyon College, as an institution, nurtured my scholarship on this project through the Whiting Teaching Fellowship and several faculty development grants that funded the archival research.

For their feedback on early drafts of this project, I am thankful to Jim Carson and Sarah Heidt, as well as to my colleagues in the Kenyon College Faculty Seminars, who took time to read and comment on my work. I also appreciated Pat Valenti's feedback on an early draft of the Peabody chapter.

For their help as early research assistants I am grateful to the wonderful Kate Kremer, Liza Chabot, and Janice Rivera-Pagán.

For their friendship, support, and their always-helpful feedback when I shared work with them, I am most appreciative to Marisa Cull and Theresa Kulbaga.

For their help with this final version, I am grateful to Pashmina Murthy and Janet McAdams. For their encouragement in getting this book done during my sabbatical, I am also thankful to Joe Klesner and Clara Román-Odio. To the anonymous readers, thank you, too!

For his superb help as my editorial assistant, my eternal gratitude goes to Liam Horsman, whose careful readings and suggestions made a world of difference on this manuscript from beginning to end.

For having carefully and patiently read this project in all its iterations, and for being my beloved *compañero* of more than two decades, mil gracias to Lance K. Oliver. To Kathleen Griffin my thanks for her amazing friendship and for always believing this day would come.

To all I have mentioned, and to everyone else who supported me in this endeavor, goes the credit for what is strong and persuasive in this project.

I, and only I, am responsible for any and all shortcomings.

INTRODUCTION

Gothic Geocultures in the Transamerican Imaginary

IN DECEMBER 2014, President Barack Obama announced that he would begin to normalize relations with Cuba to end the more than half-century-old US trade embargo imposed in October 1960 to bring down the Castro regime.[1] To mark the occasion, National Public Radio (NPR) invited Cuban-American poet Richard Blanco to suggest a "must-read" book about Cuba. Blanco chose Gustavo Pérez Firmat's *The Havana Habit*, published in 2010, noting that "the book explores the role that this island—'so near and yet so foreign'—has played in America's psychic life."[2] As articulated by Pérez Firmat, Cuba's simultaneous nearness and foreignness, along with its representation as a geography that occupies a "psychic" place in the US imaginary, is key to understanding the island's role in US literary history and culture.[3]

---

1. President Barack Obama and Cuban President Raúl Castro in 2014 announced a process to restore full diplomatic ties and to lift the full trade embargo established in 1962. In 2015, the embassies closed in 1961 reopened, and in 2016 Obama became the first sitting president to visit the island in almost ninety years. In June 2017, President Trump imposed travel and business restrictions, dialing back the Obama era's rapprochement. See Council on Foreign Relations, *U.S.-Cuba Relations*.

2. Blanco, "'Rum, Rumba, and Romance,'" 2.

3. I use the term "representation," through written and other artistic means, to signify the ways in which language produces meaning within a particular culture. Hall, *Representation*, 1.

The Havana Habit is one of the most recent books to examine the historiography of US textual and visual representations of Cuba, as well as the island's sustained cultural significance in the region. Pérez Firmat—born in Havana and raised in Miami—argues for "the centrality of Cuba" in US perceptions of Latin America, and for its "pervasive [. . .] imprint on this country's cultural landscape" (2).[4] Tracing the imprint Cuba has left on the US imagination, from the mid nineteenth century through the twentieth, and through multiple genres, such as travelogues, illustrations, films, and songs, Pérez Firmat notes how a main component of Cuba's appeal is that it "offered [US Americans] the possibility of becoming someone else elsewhere" (8). This trope of transformative influence and duality, of enabling visitors to become "someone else," is a major element of how Cuba has been represented by US writers, especially in the nineteenth century.

Because US expansionism during most of that time period was linked to slavery, representations of Cuba are also connected to it, whether in support of or against that institution. Recently, historian Edward E. Baptist has argued that "by 1850, Cuba was the one real jewel yet to be pried from the crown of the Spanish Empire," because the island was "to sugar what Mississippi [. . .] was to cotton."[5] With the liberation of the French colony of Saint-Domingue after the Haitian Revolution (1791–1804), and in the wake of substantial innovations in sugar milling by Cuban planters, the acquisition of Cuba by the United States became "essential to the South," in the view of many Southerners.[6] Economic interests in Cuban slavery, however, were not solely stoked in the South, since the North was equally implicated in the transatlantic slave trade. As historian Calvin Schermerhorn has noted:

> Hands that drew bills of exchange, graded and traded commodities, or trimmed the sails of merchant vessels were as important to the process of slaving as hands that picked cotton or those that grabbed hold of whips, grasped the throats, or groped the loins of African-descended captives.[7]

---

4. Throughout the book, I use in-text citations for primary sources and shortened citations in the footnotes for secondary sources.
5. Baptist, *The Half Has Never Been Told*, 354.
6. Baptist, *The Half Has Never Been Told*, 356.
7. Schermerhorn, *The Business of Slavery*, 3.

In the measure that slavery fueled the rise and development of capitalism, Cuba increasingly took on a protagonist role in the US imaginary, especially for Northerners (including many of the writers in this study) for whom the island became a site that produced an uneasy fascination.

The representational fixation with the island, and its presence as a cultural commonplace in US literary history, intensified during the 1840s and 1850s, when thousands of visitors traveled to Cuba. The island became a place where US Americans went to convalesce from illness (usually tuberculosis), and many also became investors in growing industries, including those powered by slave labor. Between the 1840s and 1890s, the US government tried at least five times to purchase the island from Spain, and the US fixation with Cuba was so strong that Pérez Firmat took the title of his book from the term "Havana habit," used by a US correspondent during the Spanish-American War of 1898 to describe the obsessive relationship with Cuba (24). Burgeoning US political and economic interest in Cuba was reflected in the resulting literary boom, and Pérez Firmat points to how "between 1850 and 1899, more than seventy travel books about Cuba were published in the United States" (27). The representational commonalities among these narratives are so numerous that Rodrigo Lazo has described them generically as "Cuba guides," or texts that combined "political observation with practical information on travel."[8] A majority of these works—mostly travelogues—sought to "sell" Cuba to visitors and investors, and they helped to position the island as a rhetorical commonplace in nineteenth-century US literary culture within clearly defined terms.[9]

Describing the longevity of these representational constants, Pérez Firmat adds that "American images and beliefs about Cuba have remained essentially the same for two hundred years, in spite of the social and political tempests that have battered the island" (9). Primarily, he finds that Cuba is most often signified in US texts as a "pleasure island, an Eden for the sensually deprived," a location where visitors could forget their inhibitions and indulge in making fantasies real (11). Crafted as this type of signifier, however, Cuba also functioned as a "projection," a refraction of "qualities or impulses" repressed by a collective US psyche (11). Because Cuba acted as "America's reflected self,"

---

8. Lazo, "Against the Cuba Guide," 181.
9. For an anthology of many of those accounts, see Pérez, *Slaves, Sugar, & Colonial Society*. See also Smith, "A Bibliography of American Travellers."

Pérez Firmat observes, the island was "enticing but ultimately undesirable" (11). In many textual representations, and sometimes even within the same narrative, "Cuba was paradise, and Cuba was hell" (31). This notion of Cuba's duality in its simultaneous desirability and repulsiveness, and in embodying (and reflecting back on the United States) both what was most desired and most feared, produced a conflicted literary relationship with Cuba for many US writers.

Regardless of whether they wrote positively and/or negatively about Cuba, most travelers (and even US writers who never visited the island) represented the island and/or its inhabitants in ways that reasserted US exceptionalism and justified its anticipated colonialist dominance. Indeed, as Pérez Firmat asserts, "whether glowing or damning," all appraisals of Cuba "were refracted through the lens of prospective possession" (31). Lazo has also underscored how Cuba guides "appeared alongside rhetoric about US annexation of Cuba," representing "the island as a territory in the orbit of US geopolitical and commercial interests," especially prior to the US Civil War.[10] In this way, and whether US desires and fears were political, economic, or carnal, figurations of Cuba were always already linked to the budding imperialist project throughout the 1800s.

Further, Cubans in exile living in the United States because of their opposition to Spanish colonial rule also wrote about the island, and about their experiences in the rising empire. Lazo has shown how Cuban exiles were part of a large stateside community that included important literary figures such as José María Heredia, José Martí, and Cirilo Villaverde. Indeed, by the late nineteenth century, Lazo notes, "Cuban intellectuals had been publishing in the United States for more than fifty years," and during that century produced and published more than seventy Spanish-language newspapers.[11] The work of these writers contributed to the transamerican trove of figurations within the "longstanding two-way flow of economic, political and cultural exchange between the United States and the island," which connected slavery to

---

10. Lazo, "Against the Cuba Guide," 182. Also within this context, Brickhouse has pointed to how "the confederacy [. . .] often imagined itself quite beyond the territorial borders of the nation: in relation to and as the potential seat of a Greater South, a slaveholding empire that might encompass Cuba, the Caribbean, the southern hemisphere in its entirety." Brickhouse, *Transamerican*, 7.

11. Lazo, *Writing to Cuba*, 3, 4.

US empire and to Cuba.[12] The United States reached its expansionist apex in 1898 when it declared war on Spain, invading Cuba and Puerto Rico, and thereby ending more than four centuries of Spanish colonial rule in the Caribbean.[13] Once the war over Spanish colonial possessions in the Caribbean and the Pacific ended, US interest in Cuba grew exponentially, and the fascination Pérez Firmat describes continued to build into the twentieth century and beyond.

Within this frame of reference, *Gothic Geoculture: Nineteenth-Century Representations of Cuba in the Transamerican Imaginary*, draws from Gothic, Latinx, and Hemispheric/Transamerican studies to trace specific representational patterns and shifts between the 1830s and the 1890s. While most book-length studies on representations of Cuba are US-centric, focusing mainly on the late nineteenth and twentieth centuries, this project examines a sixty-year period when the "two-way flow" included gothicized tropes of the island used by US *and* Cuban writers alike. Through notions of monstrosity, doubleness, corruption, possession, and infection, the writers in this study—William Cullen Bryant, Nathaniel Willis, Sophia Peabody, Mary Peabody Mann, Martin R. Delany, Louisa May Alcott, Cirilo Villaverde, Evangelina Cisneros, and José Martí—drew on the gothic to represent Cuba either as dangerous and/or as imperiled. Through a comparative close reading analysis of specific literary case studies, this project focuses on how these texts actively gothicized Cuba (and/or the United States) within the context of nineteenth-century empire-building and anticolonial struggle.

By utilizing the language of fear, the texts herein cautioned against or advocated for US imperialism during the time when Cuba was most wanted and dreaded as a potential colonial acquisition, from both the US and Cuban sides.[14] But by century's end, the figurative trend of

---

12. Lazo, *Writing to Cuba*, 7.
13. Foner has argued that the Spanish-Cuban-American War birthed US imperialism. See Foner, *The Spanish-Cuban-American War*. Peterson has further advocated for the title Spanish-American-Cuban-Filipino War to "represent all the major participants and to identify where the war was fought and whose interests were most at stake." Peterson, "U.S. Intervention in Cuba," 5.
14. In discussing Cuban annexationists, Lazo has noted how some "were slave owners who sought to protect their economic interests by having Cuba join the Union as a slave state." Further, some exiles "believed that if Cuba became a U.S. state, it would not face the political upheavals that had shaken many independent

gothicizing the island as pernicious shapeshifted, and Cuba was instead portrayed as a gothic heroine in need of rescue, exploiting the trope of the innocent woman preyed upon by a threatening monster or villain.[15] In studying how this group of writers used tropes of fear within the geopolitical context of battling empires, *Gothic Geoculture* takes a hemispheric view, expanding on Cuba's current representational historiography.[16] By exploring the relationship between the gothic, transatlantic slavery, and Cuba, this study also broadens our understanding of the roles the island played within the transamerican imaginary. Specifically, *Gothic Geoculture* points to elements of what we know, more globally, as the transamerican or hemispheric gothic.[17]

Through the pairing of case studies from different genres, including journals, travel narratives, essays, and fiction, this project examines representations of Cuba that conjure what I call a *gothic geoculture*. I introduce this term to identify part of the "geosocial construct" that served to codify the system of slavery in this hemisphere, and which represented race, gender, and nationality as imbricated categories that imposed epistemological (constructed) and ontological (inherent) meanings on colonially subalternized locations, such as Cuba.[18] With this idea at its core, the book is divided into five chapters, each of which defines and explores a major component of a gothic geoculture:

Latin American nations." In the antebellum period, Lazo adds, "the dominant strain in writings by Cuban exiles [. . .] is pro-United States." Lazo, *Writing to Cuba*, 5, 7. Leary has further noted how "Cuban annexation was also the co-creation of white Cuban exiles who forged an alliance with U.S. expansionists to chart a future for republicanism and for slavery." Leary, *A Cultural History*, 20.

15. Citing several examples, including Cisneros, Prados-Torreira points to how US reporters in Havana fed the public's thirst "for more stories on Cuban women as vulnerable victims of Spanish cruelty." Prados-Torreira, *Mambisas*, 138.

16. In discussing the relationship between politics and fear in anthropological terms, Cap has noted how "public leaders tend to legitimize their actions or proposals for action in terms of oppositions between right and wrong, good and evil, acceptable and unacceptable." Cap, *The Language of Fear*, 13.

17. Interested in the "hidden links between the United States and Haiti," and in de-centering "the connection between the United States and Europe," Bray has categorized the hemispheric gothic as a way "to convey a political, social, and cultural order in which multiple power dynamics are imaginable rather than fixed in relation to colonial and imperialist histories." Bray, "A Climate," 4.

18. Quijano and Wallerstein describe the Americas "as a geosocial construct [. . .] born in the long sixteenth century," and "as the constitutive act of the modern world-system." Quijano and Wallerstein, "Americanity as a Concept," 549.

- First, the figuration of Cuba as a *corruptive gothicscape*, where the island's inhabitants, along with its landscape and geography, were represented as always already infected by the system of slavery, and also as dangerously infectious;
- Second, the notion that Cuba belonged to a larger system of *gothicized souths* or a geopolitical ideation that linked the US South, Latin America, and the Caribbean in gothic terms through slavery, suggesting that geography determined a racialized and gendered destiny;
- Third, that gothicscapes became *transgressive hauntings*, or articulations of long-standing fears over transformations empowered by this geoculture, especially in relation to transgressions of gendered norms among white women;
- Fourth, that representing these spaces often depended on the *gothic emplotment* of white women's experiences as constrained between the figurative bounds of a gothic villain or a gothic victim; and,
- Finally, how this geoculture produced a counter-discourse I identify as a *decolonial transamericanity*, which sought to decolonize knowledge produced about Cuba and the Americas by drawing on similar gothicized representational patterns.[19]

In functioning as a geoculture, slavery linked disparate geographies, populations, and societies, promoting and disseminating shared "idea-systems" throughout the Americas. Slavery was not only a racialized economic engine fueled by human torture and exploitation, but also a critical element of Americanity (of the discursive structures that comprise the hemispheric concept of America), as Aníbal Quijano, Immanuel Wallerstein, Walter Mignolo, and others have argued.[20] For

---

19. I use the term geoculture as introduced by Wallerstein, and as nuanced by Mignolo, to describe an "idea-system" within specific economic, sociopolitical, and geographical/cultural contexts. Wallerstein, *Geopolitics and Geoculture*, 160. Mignolo critiques Wallerstein for describing "only the hegemonic imaginary of the modern world system as geo-culture," and for "denying the contribution of three centuries of Spanish and Portuguese power" in the hemisphere. Mignolo, "Coloniality at Large," 40, 43.

20. Quijano and Wallerstein refer to Americanity as the "gigantic ideological overlay" imposed on the Americas by the forces of empire, and its imbricated components of "coloniality, ethnicity, racism, and the concept of newness itself." Quijano

Mignolo, the fact that slavery became "synonymous with blackness [. . .] is not a description of colonialism, but of coloniality," or of how the modern world-system was discursively constructed (28). These ideological paradigms, born from slavery's contact zones, existed not only during the time of the transatlantic slave trade and after Emancipation, but also persist today. *Gothic Geoculture* engages with the particularity of one such representational element in relation to Cuba: namely, the island's literary figuration as a gothic geoculture.

This gothicization of Cuba in its relationship to the United States emerges in the geopolitical context of the transamerican imaginary, which Paula M. L. Moya and Ramón Saldívar have defined as "'transnational' to the degree that 'American' fiction must be seen anew as a heterogeneous grouping of overlapping but distinct discourses that refer to the [United States] in relation to a variety of national entities," and as "an interpretive framework that yokes together North and South America."[21] In taking a transamerican perspective, this project underscores Moya and Saldívar's point that "much American literature responds to ideological pressures from outside the geopolitical borders of the sovereign United States," and supports a reconsideration of what we mean when we describe "American" literature.[22] Within the larger framework of a transamerican imaginary, this book contributes to what Caroline Levander has described as "Cuba's constitutive importance to nineteenth-century US expansionism," and of how the island "disrupts as well as enables national fantasies of imperial mastery" through its "crucial transnational impact on US culture."[23] By moving beyond a US-centered perspective to consider how some Cuban writers used the gothic in representing themselves, the region, and/or the United States, my project engages a broader swath of the transamerican imaginary,

---

and Wallerstein, "Americanity as a Concept," 550. Mignolo has described "'coloniality' as the other side (the darker side?) of modernity," or "the side silenced by the reflexive image that modernity [. . .] constructed of itself." Mignolo, "Coloniality at Large," 22, 24.

21. Moya and Saldívar, "Fictions," 1–2.

22. Moya and Saldívar, "Fictions," 4. Building on the definition by Eduardo Glissant, who categorized the "imaginary" as "the symbolic world through which a community (racial, national, imperial, sexual, etc.) defines itself," Mignolo has further given "the term a geo-political meaning" to connect it to "the foundation and formation of the imaginary of the modern/colonial world-system." Mignolo, "Coloniality at Large," 20.

23. Levander, "Confederate Cuba," 821, 822.

thereby attending to what Lazo has named as "the multiple locations of writings that crossed languages, national borders, and sociocultural contexts."[24]

Gothic Geoculture also moves beyond existing scholarship on US representations of Cuba, which has emerged mostly from the social sciences and focused on 1898 (when the United States invaded the island), or on the post-1959 period after the Cuban Revolution.[25] Instead, this literary study spotlights the more nuanced ways in which Cuba—what Philip D. Beidler has described as the "Cuba of the cultural imagination" in both its "physical and imaginative geography"— was represented in narratives earlier in, and throughout, the nineteenth century.[26] In keeping with its hemispheric perspective, the project takes a multidirectional approach by also considering Cuban writers writing from and/or about the United States. My interest here, however, is not in making broad claims about how *most* US or Cuban writers represented Cuba and/or the United States in the nineteenth century. Instead, *Gothic Geoculture* focuses specifically on how a group of writers drew on the language of fear, mostly on gothicized tropes, within the context of nineteenth-century US imperialist ambitions toward Cuba.

The figurations of Cuba in this study are part of but also move beyond unflattering assessments common in many nineteenth-century travelogues, such as those written by authors described by Pérez Firmat as the "naysayers," who used the island primarily as a way to underscore US exceptionalism and racial superiority (29). In addition to utilizing Cuba as a foil for the United States, John Patrick Leary has pointed to how the island was "metaphorically domesticated, infantilized, Orientalized, and eroticized, in one instance praised as a splendorous, untouched Eden, then denounced as a decadent, Catholic,

---

24. Lazo, *Writing to Cuba*, 14. Silva Gruez describes her own work in tracing such "geographies" as a way "to stretch the silhouette of U.S. national identity—in both its spatial and temporal dimensions—out of recognizable shape, making way for a transnational historical framework that will accommodate the peculiar subject-position of Latinos from the nineteenth century to the twenty-first." Silva Gruez, *Ambassadors of Culture*, 13.

25. See Beidler, *The Island Called Paradise*; Pérez, *Cuba in the U.S. Imagination, The War of 1898*, and *Slaves, Sugar, & Colonial Society*; Pérez Firmat, *The Havana Habit*. See also Leary, *A Cultural History of Underdevelopment*.

26. Beidler, *The Island Called Paradise*, 1, 6.

Africanized barbarism."[27] My project is interested in how US writers gothicized Cuba in binary terms as a corruptive location to reinforce US exceptionalism, often by eliding the shared geoculture of slavery, and in how Cuba's represented duality was expressed through tropes of fear. Similarly, I examine how US influence also was figured as potentially dangerous to Cuba, thus suggesting the pernicious transamerican reciprocity of this geoculture. Further, my book explores how such representations were preoccupied with factual or impending horrors—including the torture and trauma inherent to slavery (and its legacies)—eliciting a sense of clear and present danger that could jeopardize the future of both Cuba and the United States.

In that way, *Gothic Geoculture* contributes to the study of the Global Latin/o Americas by engaging with the "overlapping histories and geographies" of the region, and with the "mutually inflecting fields," or the "complex webs of regional, national, and hemispheric forces that can be approached from multiple locations and perspectives and that can help us to reframe American cultural analysis."[28] Proposing that we consider how American slavery, in the hemispheric sense, was represented as a geoculture that influenced how Cuba was signified, this project focuses on discursive overlaps within the transamerican imaginary. By establishing ideological hierarchies in how the Americas were figured—the basis for the concept of Americanity—such imbricated systems (of race, gender, nation) constructed "subalternized identities" across the hemisphere, including the gothicized representations of Cuba in this project.[29]

Within that framework, these representations of Cuba reflect what Kirsten Silva Gruez has categorized as "the ideal of a transamerican culture—of a bridgeable, thinkable communion between the

---

27. Leary, *A Cultural History*, 37.
28. Levander and Levine, *Hemispheric American Studies*, 2, 3.
29. Saldívar, *Trans-Americanity*, xix. In proposing this structure of meaning, Saldívar expands on Quijano and Wallerstein's assertion that politics, economics, and culture in the Americas became "linked together" through the "coloniality of power," or the discursive "system of hierarchical layers" that did not end when colonial status ended. Quijano and Wallerstein, "Americanity as a Concept," 550. Saldívar adds that it "is crucial for trans-American historical sociologists and for those of us in US Latino/a studies and American studies [to acknowledge that] when the formal colonial states ended through the wars of independence and what we today call decolonization, the coloniality of power did not." Saldívar, *Trans-Americanity*, xi.

Anglophone and Hispanophone worlds," which she argues was primarily fueled "by the powerful engine of US territorial expansion."[30] This "hemispheric imaginary," and its related "transamerican sense of space," were concomitantly produced by Spain's repressive response to growing subversiveness in Cuba, something that drove many writers, including Villaverde, Martí, and Cisneros to seek refuge in the United States.[31] Anna Brickhouse has further studied how the "literary transamericanisms" created by US writers in the decades before the Civil War "struggled to reconcile the formal structures and racial ideology of literary nationalism with a distinctly transamerican imaginary shaped by cultural fantasies and anxieties about the wider Americas."[32] In describing it as a methodology, Ramón Saldívar has noted how a transamerican approach provides "a new vocabulary for naming, studying, and comparing the hemispheric Americas and their literatures."[33] In taking a transamerican view, this study is interested in the concurrently gothicized "fantasies and anxieties" about the island that arose both in the United States and in Cuba within the transamerican imaginary.[34]

Further, in moving beyond the adjective transamerican, *Gothic Geoculture* builds on José David Saldívar's notion of "trans-Americanity." Noting that the forces that shaped Americanity "did not stop at the Rio Grande," Saldívar foregrounds the significance of "the Southwestern US-Mexican borderlands (from Texas to California)" to hemispheric meaning-making.[35] Thus, he calls attention to the "cross-genealogy" of the transamerican "systems of expression" that created a "conjunctural present—where multiple times exist simultaneously within and across the same planetary location."[36] Such discursive structures func-

---

30. Silva-Gruez, *Ambassadors of Culture*, 3.
31. Silva-Gruez, *Ambassadors of Culture*, 37–38.
32. Brickhouse, who examines the thirty-year period between 1826 and 1856 as the period in which the narrative of a national literary history was developed, suggests that examining "the transamerican and multilingual literary practices of these American arenas" enables a reconsideration of nineteenth-century literary history within the practice of what she calls "literary transamericanisms." Brickhouse, *Transamerican*, 27–28.
33. Saldívar, "Comparing Modern Literatures," 200.
34. For work on the relationship between sensationalist literature and US empire, see Streeby's *American Sensations,* and her co-edited volume with Alemán on *Empire and the Literature of Sensation.*
35. Saldívar, *Trans-Americanity*, xiv.
36. Saldívar, *Trans-Americanity*, x, xix, xxviii.

tion as "conceptual axes" that not only transcend hemispheric borders, but also produce patterns of signification.[37] Centered on one such conjuncture "within and across" transamerican literary history, *Gothic Geoculture* identifies concurrent gothicized representations of Cuba and the United States as integral components of nineteenth-century transamericanity.

Proposing that slavery functioned discursively as a geoculture as part of transamericanity, my project also foregrounds how that institution was a constitutive element in the resultant system of concepts and practices that unified the hemisphere. For Matthew Pratt Guterl, these idea-systems fashioned what he identifies as "the slaveholding world of the Atlantic Mediterranean," which shared a common set of representational similarities.[38] Guterl notes how

> portraits of the South that emphasized its Caribbean flavor, of its 'eroticism,' were, implicitly or explicitly, drawing conclusions about its location in relation to the 'tropics,' conclusions that could often emphasize the relationship between hot temperatures, immorality, violence, and sex. To call the South hot-tempered or racially hybrid, in other words, was to draw attention to its history of race mixing, to make it seem 'Latin American,' and to suggest, as generations of ethnologists and climatologists would later do, that civilization could hardly survive let alone prosper beneath a certain latitude.[39]

Guterl's observation that the term "the tropics" was used to categorize the signifying chain connecting the US South, Latin America, and the Caribbean point to geographical and cultural aspects (such as slavery and its aftermaths) as main links that connect the gothicized representations that my study is concerned with.[40]

---

37. Saldívar, *Trans-Americanity*, xviii.

38. Guterl argues that "Cuba and the South had long enjoyed a special relationship as two of the largest and closest remaining slaveholding societies in the New World," and how, this, in turn, led to the "overlap and cross-pollination," to the "binding familiarities" of the "global South." Guterl, "An American Mediterranean," 100.

39. Guterl, "An American Mediterranean," 103.

40. Guterl underscores the "pan-American production, with rich and meaningful backdrops, global plotlines, and multiple angles of spectatorship," which "took place [...] in the American Mediterranean—the extraordinary network of rivers, seas, and

This focus on the components of transamericanity moves my project beyond the many groundbreaking studies focused on the British and US gothics, and on their relationship to each other. In that vein, my study answers more recent calls for "a transatlantic view of the emergence and flowering of the Gothic."[41] As Monika Elbert and Bridget M. Marshall note: "National borders cannot contain the Gothic, and indeed, the study of the development of the Gothic is richly enhanced by looking beyond such limitations."[42] Specifically, the approaches to the gothic most relevant to this project stem primarily from critical interventions by Toni Morrison, Teresa A. Goddu, Johan Höglund, and Jesse Alemán. Morrison has argued that slavery constitutes a historical and literary haunting in US literature, identifying "the shadow that is companion to this whiteness—a dark and abiding presence that moves the hearts and texts of American literature with fear and longing."[43] Expanding on that paradigm, Goddu describes the "American Gothic" as a genre that "tells of the historical horrors that make national identity possible yet must be repressed in order to sustain it."[44] More recently, Höglund identifies the "American Imperial Gothic" as that which is "concerned with the maintenance of the racial, sexual, cultural, political and territorial borders that have helped this form of culture to explain and even justify colonial expansion and the maintenance of empire."[45] *Gothic Geoculture* focuses on the juncture where the gothic and transamericanity meet, and where slavery, race, gender, and nationality become imbricated discourses that not only serve to

---

waterways that served as the lifeblood of the New World, where longstanding currents and flows shaped the deeper history of slavery and freedom." Guterl, *American Mediterranean*, 11.

41. Elbert and Marshall, *Transnational Gothic*, 1. Additional helpful edited collections on the gothic include Castillo and Crow, *The Palgrave Handbook of the Southern Gothic* (2016); Hoeveler and Heller, *Approaches to Teaching Gothic Fiction: The British and American Traditions* (2003); Hogle, *The Cambridge Companion to Gothic Fiction* (2002); Hughes, Punter, and Smith, *The Encyclopedia of the Gothic* (2016); Martin and Savoy, *American Gothic: New Interventions in a National Narrative* (2009); Punter, *A Companion to the Gothic* (2001); Spooner and McEvoy, *The Routledge Companion to Gothic* (2007); among many others.

42. Elbert and Marshall, *Transnational Gothic*, 6.
43. Morrison, *Playing in the Dark*, 33.
44. Goddu, *Gothic America*, 10.
45. Höglund, *The American Imperial Gothic*, 3.

explain and justify, but also to challenge, US imperialist expansion in the region.⁴⁶

Moving beyond a US-focused gothic toward a "trans-American" or hemispheric gothic, this project focuses on a region Alemán has described as "haunted by the specters of empire."⁴⁷ In addition, Alemán has coined the term "inter-American Gothic" to identify how "sameness rather than difference haunts the Americas and challenges us to rethink the hemisphere not as a cleft in two but as our America and the other America at the same time."⁴⁸ The inter-American Gothic reveals the "national others whose formative presence is subsequently buried (interred) but nonetheless felt and often expressed through gothic discourse."⁴⁹ Such hemispheric doubleness is also key for Russ Castronovo and Susan Gillman, who have proposed that an "American doubleness," in regional terms, "makes comparability both internal and external to the Americas, the object studied in relation to [the world], as well as to itself."⁵⁰ This shared doubleness, in temporal and spatial terms, "multiplies into a simultaneity of times, places, and languages existing unevenly across the multiple national states of the Americas."⁵¹ *Gothic Geoculture* focuses on the dualities inherent to the hemispheric gothic to show how, with regard to Cuba, what is gothicized within (and is thereby interamerican) simultaneously transcends geographical borders (and thus becomes transamerican), casting the island *both* as an internally corruptive "double" *and* as an externally threatening "monster."⁵²

---

46. Lugones has critiqued Quijano's work for its failure to address "this deep imbrication of race, gender, class, and sexuality," within the framework that she describes as "the colonial/modern gender system." Lugones notes the importance of recognizing "the extent to which the imposition of this gender system was as constitutive of the coloniality of power as the coloniality of power was constitutive of it." Lugones, "*Heterosexualism*," 187, 189, 202.
47. Alemán, "The Other Country" 2006, 410.
48. Alemán, "The Other Country" 2007, 78.
49. Alemán, "The Other Country" 2007, 79.
50. Castronovo and Gillman, *States of Emergency*, 10–11.
51. Castronovo and Gillman, *States of Emergency*, 11.
52. Bray has argued that the "hemispheric gothic calls on the United States to account for its participation in [its] bloody histories—it is always involved and always reminded of its hemispheric identity—through intertwining genealogies that intimately connect it to those nations from which [the United States] ideologically distances itself." Bray, "A Climate," 5.

More recently, and in naming the "tropical Gothic," Justin D. Edwards and Sandra Guardini Vasconcelos have identified the "literary geography of the American tropics" as encompassing "both the tropics and sub-tropics, extending from the southern region of the mainland US territories through Mexico and the Caribbean into Central and South America."[53] Focusing on different "traditions of Gothic in the region," Edwards and Guardini Vasconcelos are interested in "how North Atlantic Gothic tropes have been transported to these tropical and subtropical zones as a way of addressing the violence and inequality that 'haunts' this part of the Americas." Their specific conceptualization of a hemispheric gothic recognizes how the region has been gothicized within "the particular nature of the imperial and historical experience in this part of the world."[54] The multipronged contextualizations of the "tropical gothic," and its intentional association of literary genre with the push and pull of empire in the Americas and with the racialized/gendered/national asymmetries it produced, make this category particularly helpful when positioning the gothic in a geocultural frame. The breadth of this approach, within its particularized scope, helps to account for the different, yet concurrent and uncannily similar, representational choices some US and Cuban writers alike made when gothicizing Cuba, which *Gothic Geoculture* engages with as articulations of transamericanity.

In addition to its particular interest in the gothic, by examining literary works composed between 1830 and 1898, *Gothic Geoculture* serves as a literary "prequel" to historical and cultural scholarship on representations of Cuba immediately before and after the Spanish-American War. In addition to Pérez-Firmat and Beidler's work, historian Louis A. Pérez, Jr. has studied the ways in which US imperialism "was inscribed within cultural forms as a source of usable modes of knowledge and deployed by way of metaphorical constructs."[55] Focusing on primary historical sources, such as pre- and post-1898 political cartoons in US newspapers, Pérez argues that "the function of metaphor" in US representations of Cuba signifies the "purpose" of imperial power. He notes that when "situated within a moral system, with its attending codes of cultural conduct and social convention, metaphor

---

53. Edwards and Guardini Vasconcelos, "Tropicalizing the Gothic," 4.
54. Edwards and Guardini Vasconcelos, "Tropicalizing the Gothic," 4, 5.
55. Pérez, *Cuba in the American Imagination*, 2.

transforms moral-to-live-by into prescription-to-act-upon."⁵⁶ While Pérez has been criticized for oversimplifying the function of metaphor as a "representational machine," his detailed exploration of the ways in which Cuba was signified in these primary sources is key to finding the connection between such representations and how the island functioned as a gothic geoculture in the transamerican imaginary.⁵⁷

Indeed, Pérez's work helps us see how "the vernacular of empire" about Cuba shifted shape by century's end from the gothic specters created by writers to caution readers about the potential dangers that would result from that island's acquisition. Instead, gothic images of emaciated corpses or of women starved, shackled, or about to be murdered, were deployed to advocate for imperial expansion into Cuba without ambivalence or ambiguity. To that end, Pérez shows how the island "underwent anthropomorphic transformation" so that a "new metaphor of Cuba emerged, one that imagined Cuba as a woman and depicted the island as a victim, mostly the victim of the misdeeds of Spanish men."⁵⁸ Though the gendering of Cuba as a woman was not new, the figuration of the island in political cartoons "in plaintive pose beseeching the Americans for rescue and redemption" did signal a change in rhetoric. Such late-century representations, Pérez argues, sought to promote "notions of chivalric duty from which to infer gender-scripted obligations and culturally derived codes of conduct to act upon," all in the service of empire.⁵⁹ By the late 1890s the representation of Cuba as a woman in distress was meant to suggest that the United States should "provide protection to women or to a country—emblematically feminized—that rival [Spanish] men [were] violating."⁶⁰ Similar to how gendering Cuba as dangerously corruptive before 1898 sought to elicit fear, figurations of Cuba's feminized weakness against Spain not only articulated the patriarchal notions of coloniality, but also added to Cuba's represented duality.

---

56. Pérez, *Cuba in the American Imagination*, 13.
57. Leary has noted how "metaphor," contrary to Pérez's assertions, "does not make up a coherent ideological system but a contradictory and flexible representational practice." Leary, *A Cultural History*, 76–77. This project seeks to engage with one way in which we see the contradictions and flexibility of that representational practice.
58. Pérez, *Cuba in the American Imagination*, 71.
59. Pérez, *Cuba in the American Imagination*, 71.
60. Pérez, *Cuba in the American Imagination*, 73.

Further, the anxiety over historical and actual events, and over futurity—of the nation, the island, the hemisphere—is one of the most salient shared characteristics among the texts I focus on in *Gothic Geoculture*. The emphasis of many of these narratives on their own "factuality," and on how they reflect "real life," connects a gothicized Cuba to how the gothic was used in slave narratives. Goddu has pointed to how, in such stories, "the difficulty of negotiating the line between fact and fiction is especially apparent in [the] use of the gothic."[61] Though slave accounts are associated with "a documentary form and adherence to veracity," they also contain disturbing gothicized elements that are nonetheless factual, including "horrifying scenes of torture and entrapment, lascivious masters and innocent slave girls, and curses on many generations."[62] This uneasy relationship between what is factual and what is gothicized also becomes a crucial element in how Cuba was represented within the transamerican context.

In tracing gothicized figurations of Cuba in the transamerican imaginary, this study begins with a chapter titled "Corruptive Gothicscapes: William Cullen Bryant's *Letters of a Traveller* and Nathaniel Parker Willis's *Health Trip to the Tropics*." These two texts, written by renowned New England writers in their time—Bryant, one of the most famous nineteenth-century US poets, and Willis, one of the best-known literary editors and writers—sketch what I describe as corruptive gothicscapes produced by the geoculture of slavery. Both Bryant and Willis traveled to Cuba early in the 1850s as part of what Lazo has called the "invalid trade," and they wrote in great detail about their experiences there. I begin my study here because, while both of these authors participated in the more general "Cuba guide" tradition, their representations promote tropes of fear, such as gothicized notions of racial simulacra (namely, of racially mixed women passing as "white") and of a resulting infectious corruption. For one, Bryant and Willis begin to articulate an imbricated ideation of Cuba, one in which race, gender, and nationality were fused to signify the island's inherently dangerous nature.[63]

---

61. Goddu, *Gothic America*, 136.
62. Goddu, *Gothic America*, 136.
63. In discussing the complexities of what she describes as "the sexual economy of race" in Cuba, Karen Y. Morrison observes that "Cuban-born whites were imagined as distinct from their peninsular cousins; wealth increasingly challenged noble

Cuba's corruptive effects and its function as a type of double to the US South are the focus of chapter 2, "Gothicized Souths: Martin R. Delany's *Blake, or The Huts of America* and Louisa May Alcott's 'Pauline's Passion and Punishment.'" Like Guterl's notion of an American Mediterranean, and Alemán's internal and external gothics, the ideation of these gothicized souths linked the Americas, and did so through the geoculture of slavery.[64] This chapter examines Delany's serialized novel, *Blake, or the Huts of America* (1859–1861), and "Pauline's Passion and Punishment," the 1862 short story by Louisa May Alcott, the first to win her a major monetary prize. Although composed by US writers who never visited Cuba, these narratives extend and expand on the tropes we find associated with gothicized representations of the island in the first chapter. Their figurations, moreover, appear right before or during the US Civil War, when the clamor to acquire Cuba temporarily abated as the United States embarked in its most internecine and bloodiest military conflict to date. In Delany and Alcott's works, Cuba produces dangerous doublings in the protagonists, which conjure concurrent tropes of fear (especially in relation to white US women) in the cautionary stories they tell.

The signifiers of Cuba's perceived corruptness are expanded on in chapter 3, "Transgressive Hauntings: Sophia Peabody's *Cuba Journal* and Mary Peabody Mann's *Juanita: A Romance of Real Life in Cuba Fifty Years Ago*." In this chapter, I juxtapose the letters written home from Cuba by Sophia Peabody between 1833 and 1835 with her sister Mary's 1887 novel *Juanita,* based on Mary and Sophia's letters. In comparing these texts, I trace how Sophia's transgressive self-representations, some of which are rife with gothicized overtones of madness and corruption, were exploited by Mary in her novel so that the idea of Cuba haunts both of these texts. The works, especially through their

---

birth as a determinant of elite status; and the variety of colors and castes found within colonial Cuba often defied neat classification." Morrison, *Cuba's Racial Crucible,* 5. Further complicating the racial picture in Cuba was the fact that social classes were not only divided between white *peninsulares* (Spanish) and *criollos* (island-born) but between "African-descended free people; and enslaved people." Morrison, *Cuba's Racial Crucible,* 5.

64. Wallerstein has identified the notion of an "extended Caribbean," which delineates "the slave-based, staple-crop-producing plantation zone extending from Bahia in northern Brazil to Virginia." Cited in Mulcahy, *Hurricanes and Society,* 203, note 12.

uneasy relationship to each other, turn Cuba into a location where transgressions become a haunting, adding to the notion of the island's noxiously transformative influence, especially on US white women.

In chapter 4, "Gothic Emplotments: Cirilo Villaverde's *Cecilia Valdés* and *The Story of Evangelina Cisneros: Told by Herself*," I consider the 1882 revised and expanded version of Villaverde's famous novel, which he finished while living as an exile in the United States, and Cisneros's first-person narrative, which was published in 1895 with an introduction by Julian Hawthorne and an account by reporter Karl Decker. Hawthorne, son of Sophia Peabody and Nathaniel Hawthorne, was a correspondent in Cuba before the Spanish-American War, and was asked to write the introduction to Cisneros's story. In Villaverde's novel, the Cuban mixed-race protagonist is gothicized as corrupted and scheming, while Cisneros is whitened and emplotted (and emplots herself) as a gothic heroine, victimized by Spain and in need of rescue by the United States. The fear-based meshing of race, gender, and nationality on which these texts depend, despite their different rhetorical purposes, not only reflect the doubleness associated with Cuba— the island as paradise, the island as hell—but also turn these narratives into doubles of each other, especially in how their Cuban protagonists are figured.

Finally, in chapter 5, "'Inside the Monster': José Martí's Decolonial Transamericanity," I examine selected writings by Martí between 1891 and 1895 about the United States, specifically those in which he drew on the gothic figure of the monster and on other tropes of fantasy and fear. Martí spent the last fifteen years of his life, between 1880 and 1895, living mostly in New York City, and became the principal correspondent on the United States for many Latin American readers. In the specific US-focused writings I examine here, Martí drew on the language of fear to represent his idea of the "North," in ways that sought to decolonize dominant and stereotyped representations of Cubans and Latin Americans. But in doing so, Martí also relied on imbricated notions of race, gender, and nationality to represent the hemisphere as endangered by the United States. Martí's rhetorical choices, juxtaposed with those of his predecessors and contemporaries, reverse the ways Cuba was gothicized in previous chapters, and demonstrate the complex ways in which gothic tropes functioned within the discourses of transamericanity.

Ultimately, *Gothic Geoculture* reveals how and when—from within and from without—Cuba was represented as a gothic geoculture that functioned both as internally and externally threatening. It also was represented as a location set off against the United States to argue for the latter's exceptionalism and/or for its similarity to (or even for being worse than) Cuba, and as a gothicscape in which race, gender, and nationality were fused to raise the specter of a powerfully corruptive influence. Further, in its geocultural figuration, Cuba became a geography in which actuality—not just the ghosts of the past—threatened the futurity of the island and the United States. In naming the five conceptual axes that define its chapters—Corruptive Gothicscapes, Gothicized Souths, Transgressive Hauntings, Gothic Emplotments, and Decolonial Transamericanity—*Gothic Geoculture* explores Cuba's protagonist role in nineteenth-century discourses of transamericanity. The narratives in this study span the time period that witnessed the rise of abolitionist sentiment, the ferment over emancipation before and during the US Civil War, and the abolition of slavery (first in the United States and more than two decades later in Cuba). But even though the discursive structures that signified the geoculture of slavery within transamericanity were used throughout the nineteenth century for different purposes by a diverse group of writers in the United States and Cuba, gothicized figurations remained as consistent tropes, signaling the relevance of these representations to our understanding of this period.[65]

---

65. The turn away from a US-centric to hemispheric "American Studies" began with the works of New Americanists in the 1990s. Significant influences on my own scholarship include Kaplan and Pease's edition of *Cultures of United States Imperialism,* Rowe's *Literary Culture and U.S. Imperialism,* Rowe's edition of *Post-Nationalist American Studies,* and Kaplan's *The Anarchy of Empire in the Making of U.S. Culture.*

CHAPTER ONE

Corruptive Gothicscapes

William Cullen Bryant's *Letters of a Traveller* and
Nathaniel Parker Willis's *Health Trip to the Tropics*

WILLIAM CULLEN BRYANT (1794–1868), known in the nineteenth century as "America's foremost poet," first traveled to Cuba in 1849 as part of a trip through the US South and published his *Letters of a Traveller: Notes of Things Seen in Europe and America* in 1850.[1] In recounting his experiences, one of the first observations he makes is how the island's slower pace tempts him: "I find that it requires a greater effort of resolution to sit down to the writing of a long letter in this soft climate than in the country I have left. I feel a temptation to sit idly, and let the grateful wind from the sea, coming in at the broad windows, flow around me" (174). By noting how he struggles to accomplish his work—of writing accounts about Cuba for the *New York Evening Post*—Bryant establishes a binary opposition between "the country" he left and the island, where the wind that gratifies him also naturalizes his decision not to write as the right response to his new environs. In Bryant's representation, he sets Cuba's allure in opposition to his US work ethic, and assigns a transformative influence to the island.

In uncannily similar ways, Nathaniel Parker Willis (1806–1867), who traveled through the US South and to Cuba in 1852, writes that

---

1. Muller, *William Cullen Bryant*, 1, 208.

the island numbs "the soul" in his *Health Trip to the Tropics,* published in 1854.[2] Describing a military mass where he saw Cuban society gathered in Havana, Willis notes "the atmosphere of calm and conscious intoxication which belongs to the climate," and how it "seemed, somehow, strangely preferable (for once in a way) to a New England April morning of the same date" (292). This "strange" alteration—of suddenly preferring the unfamiliar to the familiar—speaks to a corruptive effect, as Willis adds that while the "whole ceremony was an abominable profanation of the Sabbath—[. . .] I record it and my enjoyment of it, as one of those incidents and influences which, in these latitudes, be-chloroform the soul of the traveller" (292). Articulating a feeling of estrangement from New England customs while in Cuba, Willis notes how these experiences anesthetize not only his moral compass but also that of all US visitors, naturalizing that reaction as inherent to these "latitudes."

Within the trove of nineteenth-century travelogues about Cuba, Bryant and Willis's works stand out not only because of their authors' renown, but also because their narratives move beyond a usual focus on agricultural and demographic data. Louis A. Pérez's anthology, *Slaves, Sugar, & Colonial Society: Travel Accounts of Cuba, 1801–1899,* shows how many nineteenth-century writers who went to Cuba wrote about the island in analogous ways by focusing on the institution of slavery. Thematically divided, Pérez's edited collection is comprised of excerpts from thirty-five travelogues, including other renowned writers, such as Richard Henry Dana, Jr.'s *A Vacation Voyage* (1859) and Julia Ward Howe's *A Trip to Cuba* (1860). Pérez reproduces his curated narratives without analytical commentary, but the section on "Slaves and Slavery" reflects remarkable consistency among US writers who included financial and actuarial statistics related to slavery. Many wrote in detail about the value of slaves, about the number of slaves compared to the white population, and about the manner in which slaves were treated, especially on the sugar plantations, often comparing

---

2. Smith and Hughes have discussed how the "conflation of opposites [. . .] enables a Gothic collapse between living/dead, human/non-human, and self/other. This model of collapse also underpins the process in which the colonizing subject is displaced in its confrontation with racial otherness, and otherness that is both strange, distanced and exotic, and yet the site upon which racial, psychological and sexual anxieties are projected." Smith and Hughes, *Empire and the Gothic,* 3.

Cuba to the US South. Pérez does not include Bryant or Willis's works, but his anthology helps to situate these two authors within a wider literary and historical tradition, as well as to demarcate how their representations of Cuba were similar and also differed from those of their contemporaries.

Like other US writers on Cuba, Bryant and Willis express concerns about slavery on the island and its influence on the United States (and vice versa). But, differently, they articulate anxieties about how the geoculture of slavery shaped Cuba's inhabitants, and associate the latter with the same troubling influence they identify in relation to the tropical climate. Bryant and Willis draw on plot and characterization to bring people and places to life, creating remarkably similar portraits. Rodrigo Lazo has categorized the representational constancies among nineteenth-century accounts of the island generically as "Cuba guides," adding that the island's attractiveness resulted in "dozens of nineteenth-century books and articles about Cuba," which ranged from "dreamy, orientalist vision[s]" to those with "sardonic analysis and jaded tone."[3] Within that representational spectrum, I focus here on how Bryant and Willis portrayed Cuba as a *corruptive gothicscape*, my term for the way in which they figured the island's geography, climate, culture, landscape, and inhabitants as inextricably bound together and thereby raised concerns about its negative influence.[4]

This idea of a gothicscape as an element of transamericanity names the narrative trope that implicitly blended geographical location and people to codify them both as dangerous. By codifying Cuba as corruptive, these writers constructed something like what Sharon Rose Yang and Kathleen Healy have described as a "gothic landscape," or a location into which "the social, psychological, and spiritual" were collapsed together.[5] Further, the narratives also articulate gothic fears of corruption, which in the context of coloniality were linked to anxieties that colonized locations would lead colonizers to "go native," resulting in

---

3. Lazo, *Writing to Cuba*, 9.
4. Mishra has defined the "Gothicscape" as locations that produce a struggle between "despondency and madness," and as "scapes [that] defy all logic, [which] insinuate an unreal world, a simulacral, nightmarish domain of uncanny resemblances," thereby producing "narratives of excess." Mishra, "The Gothic Sublime," 292, 294, 301.
5. Yang and Healy, *Gothic Landscapes*, 2.

personal and societal regressions.[6] Justin Edwards and Sandra Guardini Vasconcelos argue that "for the colonist, the 'settling' of the 'unsettled' land brings with it a sense of the uncanny wherein the homely blurs into the unhomely," creating "an unstable ground."[7] The fear of retrogression produced by contagion from the geoculture of slavery in Cuba is at the core of the gothicscape constructed by Bryant and Willis in their travel narratives.

In fashioning Cuba as corruptive, Bryant and Willis gothicized aspects of the island in ways that contributed to what Mary Louise Pratt has described as the "shared repertoires of devices and conventions" in travel narratives.[8] Specifically, these related repertoires and conventions emerged from the larger geocultural continuum created by slavery in the Americas within the overarching discourses of transamericanity. In framing Cuba as a gothicscape, Bryant and Willis employed four main thematic structures to signify the island:

- as a site of temptation and corruption through its climate and through the related behavior of its inhabitants, cast in opposition to US culture and mores;
- as a destabilizing location where spectacle and theatricality prevailed at the expense of human sensibility and morality, especially through simulacra of whiteness that blurred the line between racialized categorizations;
- as a geography infected by the "Black Legend," which established a cautionary kinship between Cuba and the often gothicized discourses originally disseminated against Spain;[9] and
- as an exotic locale within the larger region of the "tropics," where race, gender, and nationality were fused as ontological components

---

6. Brantlinger, *Rule of Darkness*, 230.
7. Edwards and Guardini Vasconcelos, "Tropicalizing the Gothic," 2.
8. Pratt, *Imperial Eyes*, 11.
9. Brickhouse has described this discursive structure, "propounded initially in British and then in Anglo-American writings on the Spanish Conquest of the Americas," as the "set of historical narratives and perspectives that cast Spanish conquistadors as bloodthirsty Catholic villains who preyed mercilessly upon the hemisphere's indigenous races." Brickhouse, *Transamerican*, 75.

of the island's character, raising troubling concerns about its possible annexation to the United States.[10]

This construction of Cuba as a gothicscape is one of the "systems of expression" within transamericanity that disseminated supposedly inherent simultaneities within and across the hemisphere in relation to Atlantic slavery and its legacies.[11]

Bryant, born near the Berkshires in western Massachusetts, was known as the "most distinguished newspaper editor" in the nineteenth century after heading the *New York Evening Post* for five decades.[12] In his travels through the South, and after finding that his antislavery editorials had made him persona non grata to Southerners, Bryant moved on to Cuba, which he had dreamed of visiting for over a quarter century.[13] In the 1820s and 1830s, Bryant had met exiled Cubans during his stay with a Cuban family in New York, had learned Spanish, and had even translated the poem "The Hurricane" by Cuban poet José María Heredia (among about twenty poems Bryant translated from Spanish).[14] Kirsten Silva Gruez notes that Bryant's translation of Heredia's poem "was probably better known than any other Spanish American poem."[15] Further, because Bryant had written about Cuba, "the translation was often misattributed as an original poem of his own composition."[16] In 1829, Bryant had published "A Story of the Island of

---

10. In expressing anxieties about what they represented as simulacra of whiteness in Cuban society (or about what is known historically through Latin America as *blanqueamiento*), Bryant and Willis both observed, from their specific positionality, what Karen Y. Morrison has historicized as the "Cuban flexibility in racial classification" within a "shifting" system, where "transformative actions included those of white fathers who openly recognized their mixed race children, [and] women of color who bore offspring who received white jural classification." Morrison, *Cuba's Racial Crucible*, 166, 171.
11. Saldívar, "Trans-Americanity," xviii, xxviii.
12. Muller, *William Cullen Bryant*, 1, 2, 5.
13. Muller, *William Cullen Bryant*, 209.
14. Muller, *William Cullen Bryant*, 209, Silva Gruez, *Ambassadors of Culture*, 36.
15. Silva Gruez identifies Bryant, who returned to Cuba in 1872 on his way to Mexico, as one in a "trinity" of poets (along with Heredia and Maria Gowen Brooks) who enacted "a particular kind of hemispheric imaginary, processing their notions of the American sublime in a way that evades simple North/South dyads." Moreover, she notes how these poets helped craft a "transamerican sense of space" within the context of US coloniality in the region. Silva Gruez, *Ambassadors of Culture*, 36–38.
16. Silva Gruez, *Ambassadors of Culture*, 37.

Cuba," believed to have been told to him by a guest of the family he lived with in New York, since he had not yet visited the island. Anna Brickhouse argues that the tale "is also self-consciously *about* the inter-American creating and passing of narratives, and it reads, accordingly, as a kind of analogue for the acts of literary transmission informing Bryant's career."[17] In that way, Bryant was an active and influential participant within the "two-way flow" of discourses related to Cuba in the transamerican imaginary.

Willis, his younger contemporary, hailed from Portland, Maine, and also became a renowned poet, foreign correspondent, and magazine editor, widely recognized as "the most popular magazinist in America" after founding *The American Monthly* while still in his twenties.[18] In addition, Willis worked as a foreign correspondent for the *New York Mirror*, traveling through Europe and writing more than one hundred letters about his travels abroad.[19] After establishing the *Home Journal* in 1846, he famously defended Edgar Allan Poe's legacy upon the latter's death in 1849. He became involved in a scandalous divorce lawsuit that resulted in his being physically assaulted by the aggrieved husband, which prompted Willis to travel through the US South and to Cuba for health reasons. Willis's renown was linked not only to the more than twenty books he wrote throughout his life, but also to how he was represented by two women authors of his time. In 1854, his sister, Sara Payson Willis, featured a scathing caricature of him in her roman-à-clef *Ruth Hall*, which she authored under the pen name "Fanny Fern."[20] He also was unflatteringly represented in Harriet Jacobs's 1861 autobiographical but pseudonymous *Incidents in the Life of a Slave Girl*, since he employed the escaped slave as a nursemaid for his children from 1842 to 1861.[21]

After setting the tone about Cuba's seductiveness discussed above, both Bryant and Willis train their critical gazes on the women. In Bryant's account, he focuses not only on their physical bodies but also on how they embody what he represents as a problematic imbrication of race, gender, and nationality. After noting how "the women of Cuba

---

17. Brickhouse, "A Story of the Island," 9.
18. Beers, *Nathaniel Parker Willis*, 2.
19. Baker, *Sentiment & Celebrity*, 74.
20. Beers, *Nathaniel Parker Willis*, 274, 308, 318, 334.
21. Barker, *Sentiment & Celebrity*, 4.

show no tokens of delicate health," Bryant remarks on their "plump figures," and their "well-developed bust," adding how "as they advance in life, the chest, in the women particularly, seems to expand from year to year, till it attains an amplitude by no means common in our country" (174). Fixing his unabashed gaze on the women's breasts, which he comments on repeatedly, Bryant objectifies their body parts, theorizing that their physiognomy and "their general health" result from "the free circulation of air through their apartments" (174). This pseudoscientific appraisal links racial characteristics to climate (and even to architectural design), underscoring the notion that the Cuban women's uncommon bodies (as represented by Bryant) are produced by the island's geoculture.²²

Bryant also racializes the "complexion" of Cuban women, focusing on the lengths he says they go to make themselves appear whiter to suggest that they perform (rather than personify) whiteness. During an outing on a "bright moonlight night," Bryant is "surprised at seeing around me so many fair brows and snowy necks" (176). He wonders whether the effects of the moonlight or of the women's "white dresses" create this impression, "for the complexions of these ladies seem to differ several shades from those which I saw yesterday at the churches" (176). By noting how the women's skin tones, which were "fair" and "snowy" under the unreliable moonlight, are much darker in the light of day, Bryant calls attention to the distinction between artifice and actuality. He explains that a "female acquaintance" revealed to him that this whitening effect is produced by the use of "cascarilla," a "favorite cosmetic on the island," made from pulverized egg shells that are then "plastered" over a woman's face. Bryant quotes his source as noting that "I have seen a dark-skinned lady as white almost as marble at a ball" (174). In this way, Bryant supports his observation by ventriloquizing through an informant to invest his racialized representation of Cuban

---

22. Mulvey's findings on theorizing the "male gaze" in the context of narrative film are helpful in that she finds that in "a world ordered by sexual imbalance, pleasure in looking has been split between active/male and passive/female. The determining male gaze projects its phantasy on to the female figure which is styled accordingly. In their traditional exhibitionist role women are simultaneously looked at and displayed, with their appearance coded for strong visual and erotic impact so that they can be said to connote *to-be-looked-at-ness*. Woman displayed as sexual object is the leit-motif of erotic spectacle. [. . .] The presence of woman is an indispensable element of spectacle." Mulvey, "Visual Pleasure," 19.

women with seemingly objective factuality. In doing so, he depicts these women as duplicitous since they attempt to pass for white, suggesting that the performance of whiteness is widely accepted and even expected in Cuban society, which suggests that racial categorizations are not dependable.

Along the same lines, Willis pays close attention to the island's women and connects their representation to what he perceives as the spectacle of Cuban culture. In that vein, Willis begins his first letter on his visit to Havana with the description of the military mass on a Sunday morning. In addition to promoting the idea of Cuba's benumbing influence, Willis focuses his gaze on the women alighting from their carriages at the church door, noting the "magnificently elaborate [. . .] full ball dresses," adding how these "unbonneted and bare-shouldered worshippers" look "so ready for conquest" that the service itself appears like it should be happening "after a ball" (278). Willis calls attention to a sharp dissonance between the event—a religious Mass—and the way the women dress and act—as for a social spectacle aimed at sexual conquest—noting that "the rather festal costumes and surroundings, has no very devout aspect for a stranger" (278). Like Bryant, Willis creates a binary opposition between the Cubans and "a stranger," highlighting the feeling of uncanniness that Cuban culture, especially women's behavior, elicits in him. Both Bryant and Willis articulate how the island produces a sense of estrangement in relation to US culture, positioning the Cubans as racial and cultural "Others" within a US context.

Also, when focusing his gaze on the Cuban women, Willis—like Bryant—racializes their bodies, separating the objects of his scrutiny from the ideal of US womanhood in his mind's eye. Willis describes how the Cuban women alight from their *volantes* (the fast, small horse-drawn carriages that Cubans used to get around Havana), noting how "everything around contributed to the effect of those tranquil dark eyes and un-lustrous ivory of those plump shoulders—for plump is every woman in Cuba" (281). Willis's representation, which employs a more sardonic tone than Bryant's, portrays Cuban women as racially tainted. The suggestion here is that while these women look white, they are actually marred in racial terms. The related comment on their "plumpness" further demonstrates the cultural judgment Willis renders by setting a US standard (of lustrous whiteness and physical slimness) against which Cuban women do not measure up.

Exemplars of what Pratt has described as "the seeing-man," or the "male subject [...] whose imperial eyes passively look out and possess" through their travel writing, Bryant and Willis do not coincidentally target Cuban women to racialize their gender.[23] Employing an intersectional approach in her analysis of slavery, Sally L. Kitch has proposed the terms "racialized gender" or "genderized race" to describe the ways in which the institution "shifted [its foundation] from an issue of culture or religion to one of racial destiny—a bodily fate."[24] Kitch notes how race and slavery were defined "via women's bodies" through the *partus sequitur ventrum* ("status-of-the-mother") laws, at the same time that black men were "de-masculated" through denial of "the masculine prerogatives of heading a household or determining the domicile of their wives and progeny."[25] By focusing derogatorily on women's bodies, especially in contrasting them against US white women's bodies, Bryant and Willis participated in the discourses that linked "racial domination and prurience" within the geoculture of slavery, and established such representations as elements of the Cuban gothicscape.[26]

In addition, Bryant links his representation of women in terms of spectacle and artifice to horror and the grotesque in his description of the public torture and execution of a slave. In this letter, titled "Negroes in Cuba.—Indian Slaves," Bryant describes how he heard that "a negro was to suffer death early the next morning by the garrote, an instrument by which the neck of the criminal is broken and life extinguished in an instant" (189). He narrates how he asks his landlady what crime the slave committed, and she answers that the slave killed his old master while the latter was sleeping. Bryant enquires whether the slave "received any provocation," and she replies, "not that I have heard" (189). Bryant then describes, in great detail, the gory purpose of the garrote, a device designed to "push forward an iron bolt against the back of the neck [of the slave] and crush the spine at once" (189). In the same way that Bryant articulates little emotion or interest about the circumstances that led the slave to murder, Bryant's description of the garrote is detached in tone, suggesting a more ethnographic than affective interest.

---

23. Pratt, *Imperial Eyes*, 7.
24. Kitch, *The Specter of Sex*, 79.
25. Kitch, *The Specter of Sex*, 81, 85.
26. Kitch, *The Specter of Sex*, 89.

But while he does not appear particularly concerned about the slave to be executed, Bryant is detailed in his description of the crowd, especially the women. In that passage, he adds adjectives and descriptors that create a sense of place, of those who were present, and even of the weather, describing "sentinels in uniform walking to and fro, keeping the spectators at a distance from the platform, as well as the intense heat of the sun, for the sea-breeze had not yet sprung up as the crowd had begun to assemble" (189). Bryant focuses on a group of young girls who stand near to the platform, two of whom are dressed in white. He remarks on one as being "pretty," and notes how they had "no other shade for their dusky faces than their black veils, chatting and laughing and stealing occasional glances at the new-comers" (189). He is intentional in his description of the women, their contrasting attire between the white dress and dark veils, their racialized characteristics, and their behavior, in far more detail than what he tells the reader about the impending execution, or the slave to be executed. In this way, Bryant wants the reader to focus on the dissonance in the reaction of the Cuban women, even as young girls, to a sensational and cruel event that he suggests should cause some degree of revulsion in any sensible observer.

But, as the condemned "negro" takes his place on the garrote, Bryant's descriptions show that he is fascinated by the theatricality that he represents as permeating Cuban culture, where nearly everything becomes a source of entertainment. He shifts his gaze again toward the crowd to give the reader a sense of their reaction, and notes how

> a multitude of all ages and both sexes, took possession of the places from which the spectacle could be best seen. A stone-fence, such as is common in our country, [. . .] upheld a long row of spectators. A well-dressed couple, a gentleman in white pantaloons, and a lady elegantly attired, with a black lace veil and a parasol, bringing their two children and two colored servants, took their station by my side [. . .]. (190)

That a well-to-do family has come to witness the execution, and dressed up for the event, reveals the widely accepted purpose that this disciplinary display has in Cuban culture. Bryant remarks on its didactic value, noting how the black slave hoists the youngest of the children, who is about four years old, so "that it might have the full benefit of the spectacle" (190). Bryant suggests that the spectacularized punishment is meant to underscore for both the white Cuban child, as well as for the slave hoisting him, the violent racial hierarchy created by the geoculture of slavery.

Further, Bryant sets himself apart from the Cuban spectators by contrasting their matter-of-fact attitude with his own horror and dismay at witnessing the event. Bryant states:

> I had never seen, and never intended to see an execution, but the strangeness of this manner of inflicting death, and the desire to witness the behavior of an assembly of the people of Cuba on such an occasion, had overcome my previous determination. The horror of the spectacle now caused me to regret that I made one of a crowd drawn to look at it by an idle curiosity. (190)

If Bryant's narrative began with the notion of being seduced by Cuba's climate into idleness, here that transformation leads him, against his better instincts and judgment, to engage in behavior that ultimately shames him. Bryant suggests that, despite the sense of acculturation that his decision to watch the execution appears to signal, his US sensibilities prevail since he represents himself as being the only one dismayed by what he witnesses. Although he is initially drawn to what is culturally unfamiliar, wishing to learn more about the Cuban people, he is ultimately repelled and revolted by this experience, creating a clear opposition between his own reaction and that of the Cubans he portrays. In that way, while Bryant represents himself as initially corrupted by Cuban culture, his singularized regret and guilt articulate his superiority over the Cuban people.

In comparable ways, Willis focuses on the corruptive power of spectacle in his description of the military mass he witnesses when he notes how, at the same time the religious service is in process, the military band begins to play music, establishing a dissonance between piety and entertainment. Remarking on this dichotomy, Willis says:

> I must confess to an instinctive impulse to escape before the roof should fall in—sinners that we were even to listen to such music in such a place! It was really too profane, too contrary to the proper

> spirit of the spot if it were for artistic effect and propriety alone, leaving higher standards out of the question, and its formal repetition every Sunday, and the fashionable attendance, show the established religion of the island to be reduced to a level with its gayeties. (289)

His statement that "higher standards" cannot be expected builds on the notion that in Cuba the border between morality and immorality—between piety and "gayeties"—is not recognized. Although Willis notes that seeing people leaving the church "is, anywhere, something of a show," it is in Havana that the close of the Mass "is a lively spectacle indeed" (289). Thereby, Willis implies that the culture as a whole, even during a solemn religious event, is staged to create a sensory impact, one that registers as an overload for the cultural outsider-observer.

In gothicizing Cuba in these ways, Bryant and Willis also drew on the discursive structures of the "Black Legend," or the "anti-Spanish sentiments in the United States that could be traced back to Europe and a tradition of anti-Catholicism among Protestants in the Americas."[27] As Lazo points out, this sixteenth-century discourse that "portrayed Spaniards as fanatically cruel and greedy in their conquest of the Americas" was easily "transferred" in the United States to racialize "Others" and deployed "to create stereotypes and portray people of Latin American descent as evil."[28] Further, such figurations fomented "a binary division between Anglo-American and Spanish/Latin American attitudes and predispositions," which disseminated beliefs "in Anglo-American superiority [as] part of the ideology of Manifest Destiny."[29] Against this backdrop of empire, Maria DeGuzmán has argued that "figures of Spain have been central to the dominant fictions of 'American' exceptionalism, revolution, manifest destiny, and birth/rebirth: to Anglo-America's articulation of its empire as antiempire (the 'good' empire that is not one); and to its fears of racial contamination and hybridity."[30] In that way, representations of Spain and Spaniards became

---

27. Lazo, *Writing to Cuba*, 85.
28. Lazo, *Writing to Cuba*, 86.
29. Lazo, *Writing to Cuba*, 86. John L. O'Sullivan was the newspaper and magazine editor who coined the term "Manifest Destiny" to articulate US imperialist ambitions and actions in the hemisphere as justifiable and fated. Cirilo Villaverde, whose work I examine in chapter 4, met and collaborated with O'Sullivan on articles that supported filibustering in Cuba. See Lazo, *Writing to Cuba*, 171.
30. DeGuzmán, *Spain's Long Shadow*, xiii.

part of the "double movement" between "repulsion" and "romancing," or of the duality associated with racial Others as an integral element of transamericanity. In addition to this implicit doubleness, DeGuzmán has shown how the relationship between US gothic fiction and "the darkness and blackness to the figure of the Spaniard was not only a religious, ethical, and historical evaluation, but increasingly became a racial typology was well."[31] This association between Cuba and the Black Legend—a long-standing racialized paradigm that gave Spain a primary role within the gothic—is a significant element in how Bryant and Willis gothicize the island and its people.

Within the contours of the "Black Legend," and of the theatricality both Bryant and Willis represent, their narratives show the troubling effects of Cuba on US white women when exposed to the island's cultural practices. Similar to Willis's spectacularized Mass, Bryant provides a sensationalized depiction of his visit to the Havana cemetery, or Campo Santo, which further represents the island as a site of excess and dislocation. In his description of this scene, Bryant uses graphically grotesque and gothicized terms to describe how the poor were buried in a common grave. He states:

> I saw where the spade had divided the bones of those who were buried there last, and thrown up the broken fragments, mingled with masses of lime, locks of hair, and bits of clothing. Without the walls was a receptacle in which the skulls and other larger bones, dark with the mould of the grave, were heaped. (177)

This figuration is compounded by Bryant noting that the cemetery is located next to "a mad-house," as he adds that from this "long building" the "inmates, exasperated at the spectacle before them, were gesticulating from the windows—the women screaming and the men shouting, but no attention was paid to their uproar" (177). The gruesome scene of dismembered body parts, paired with the unsettling ruckus of the patients in the mental hospital, give Bryant's description a gothicized tone, but not one that perturbs the Cubans at the cemetery.

In contrast, he represents non-Cuban women as imperiled by their exposure to this gothicscape by setting the behavior of the Cubans at

---

31. DeGuzmán, *Spain's Long Shadow*, xiii, xxviii.

the Campo Santo in opposition to that of a "lady," whom he further identifies as "a stranger to the island." After visiting the cemetery and witnessing the spectacle, this woman "was so affected by the sights and sounds of the place, that she was borne out weeping and almost in convulsions" (177). This concurrent representation of the ghastly cemetery and the mayhem in the insane asylum is further gothicized by the hysteria it produces in the woman "stranger," who (in Bryant's figuration) shows the appropriate susceptibility to the disturbing and morbid scene. That this "lady" is physically and psychologically affected by her visit to the Campo Santo underscores the vulnerability of white women's sensibilities within the island's corruptive gothicscape.

Likewise, and in highlighting how "American ladies have a new experience in Havana," Willis derides Spanish and Cuban men as inferior and figures them as synonyms of each other. To advance the idea that US women are culturally (and morally) unprepared for what the island has in store for them, Willis describes a "very lovely group of the invalid pilgrims who come with every winter to this latitude." He then narrates how "two or three of the little elegantly-dressed duodecimo Spaniards walked around, and planting themselves in front, looked deliberately into their bonnets, as you would look into the open pane of a post-office window" (290). In a mocking tone, Willis portrays the men who gaze upon the US women in racialized terms, describing them as "Spaniards," and infantilizing them as "little" and as "duodecimo."[32] The US women, he says, react by initially raising "their hands to their faces, or [by turning] an inquiring look to their companions, evidently thinking the gentleman may have seen a wasp or tarantula—lip or cheek in danger, to call for such close investigation" (290). Willis adds that while only a concern for the women's safety could explain why the men openly stare at them, when that possibility is discarded and "the stare continue[s]," the visiting women turn "their backs with evident surprise and displeasure" (290). The negative reaction of the US women to the local men's scrutiny underscores what Willis has suggested before: not only that Cubans behave in hyperboli-

---

32. DeGuzmán has argued that the racialized binary opposition between Spain and the United States in the nineteenth century was significant "in the formation of Anglo-American national identity with imperial ambitions." DeGuzmán, *Spain's Long Shadow*, 139.

cally strange ways, but also that their behavior clashes with the expectations of US visitors, especially those of white women.

Still, despite his attention to the cultural divide between Cubans and US tourists, Willis celebrates what he describes as the lack of dissembling among island inhabitants, and fuses the physical with the cultural by stating that this is a "peculiarity in the physiognomy of this people" (291). Elaborating on the islanders' gaze, Willis notes: "There is no dodge in the Spanish eye. In man or woman, it comes round to you as fair and square as the side of a decanter—fearless and unwinking as an open inkstand. It has nothing to conceal or to avoid" (291). That the "Spanish" gaze is the same in men and women establishes a troubling similarity between genders, one that Willis perceives as inviting the outsider-observer to impose his own interpretation, like ink that serves no purpose until a pen writes with it. Indeed, Willis is not paying a compliment by representing the racialized gaze as "coming round," like a bottle aimed at the side of the head, or of having a blank openness. He does call this "a very great beauty," and says he is "sorry for the twenty reasons why it cannot be a peculiarity of a 'fast' country like ours" (291). But his praise seems ironic here since his description sets up the "Spanish eye" as lacking tact and thereby reflecting an uncivilized manner in keeping with the discursive constructs of the "Black Legend."

Contrary to his expressed admiration for this "unsuspicious eye" among Cubans, Willis's own gaze is largely unforgiving. When returning to the topic of the island men's stature, Willis states: "Owing, it is said, to early initiation, as children, into the unbridled license of plantation life, to excessive smoking and to intermarriage of the same race through many generations—to these causes more than to climate—the Cuban gentlemen are the most miniature aristocracy in the world" (279). Willis relies on an imprecise "it is said" to support his own pseudoscientific claim that the short stature of Cuban men (no longer Spanish here and thereby establishing a kind of interchangeable identity between Spain and Cuba) is due to inbreeding. Thereby, Willis suggests a biological malformation that conflates race, gender, and nationality within the geoculture of slavery. He adds to this figuration by stating, "They are so universally small that a promenade in Havana is like taking a walk in [sic] Liliput—or so it strikes you if you come suddenly upon an Englishman or an American of the ordinary size, and are thus reminded of the contrast" (279). Willis's reference to Jonathan Swift's *Gulliver's Travels* (1726) further establishes the colonial asymmetry, since he represents himself as Gulliver, who becomes a giant in Lilliput.[33] This juxtaposition reminds readers of the implied and inherent inferiority of the Cubans, especially when "contrasted" with US white men like him, which promotes the discursive structures of Anglo-American superiority.

After differentiating themselves from and establishing themselves as superior to the Cubans they describe, Bryant and Willis address the system of slavery and the island's possible annexation to the United States. Bryant transitions from the scene of the garrote (a torture identified with the Spanish Inquisition) into a discussion of slavery in Cuba, one in which he also addresses the treatment of indigenous peoples from the Yucatan and of Asian laborers, brought to the island to work the sugar cane fields.[34] In doing so, Bryant strikes a different tone from that in his discussion of slaves, which is rather devoid of emotion, while expressing strong indignation about the enslavement of the Indians. In keeping with the ideological underpinnings of the "Black Legend" as born from the mistreatment of indigenous peoples by the Spanish, Bryant discusses the regulation of how many times Indians may be whipped and decries: "Such is the manner in which the government of Cuba sanctions the barbarity of making slaves of the freeborn men of Yucatan" (192). In addressing race, Bryant adds that the "prejudice of color is by no means so strong here as in the United States," noting how some "mulattoes" have achieved great social mobility, and how "the government favors emancipation" because Spanish law allowed slaves to purchase their own freedom (193). Using this example to support his impression—like many other Cuba travelogues did—Bryant notes that "it is manifest that if the slave trade could be checked, and these laws remain unaltered, the negroes would gradually emancipate themselves" (193). The contrast here is clear between his outrage at the "barbarity" of enslaving indigenous "freeborn men," and his passive acceptance of the gradual emancipation argument on Cuban slavery.

---

33. Hawes has discussed how Gulliver's travels to Lilliput are marked by "an ironic appropriation of colonial discourse." Hawes, "Three Times Round the Globe," 199.

34. For more on the history of the garrote, see Paraskovich, *The Wrong View*, 140–42.

Further, not only does Bryant elide the connection between US and Cuban slavery (even as he represents US racism as worse than Cuba's), but the contrast also points to how he naturalizes the long-standing racialized hierarchies of the "Black Legend," which blamed Spain for the bloodthirsty genocide of indigenous peoples in the Americas.[35]

In representing Cuban slavery as more benevolent than that in the United States, Bryant also disseminates a recurrent observation in Cuba travelogues, which figured the island as a "better" location for slaves because Spanish laws were supposedly more humane. US writers tended to note how Cuban slavery was more benevolent because of the legalized practice of *coartación*, or manumission, through which slaves could purchase themselves.[36] Dana speaks to how Cuban "laws also directly favor emancipation," as "every slave has a right to go to a magistrate and have himself valued, and on paying the valuation, to receive his free papers." The abolitionist Howe also describes manumission by noting how the "slave laws of Cuba are far more humane than our own."[37] Historical data does show that "coartación provided an avenue for self-emancipation and created an intermediate status between slave and free."[38] However, evidence also suggests that the actual number of *coartados* in Havana was infinitesimally small (representing about one percent of the total enslaved population in 1871).[39] In contrast, many travelers also mention the fact that the lifespan of Cuban slaves did "not exceed seven or eight years."[40] This tension, between perception and fact, inherent to the geoculture of slavery, produces a troubling influence not lost on Bryant.

Bryant concludes his discussion of slavery by addressing the desire for "annexation," and again ventriloquizes an opinion through an anonymous European source, who speaks of how annexation would not be the best for Cuba. Bryant notes: "You hear something now and

---

35. Brickhouse points out how while "publicly opposed to slavery throughout his career, Bryant was nevertheless unable to imagine [US] complicity in the very triangular trade that so firmly established itself at the center of economic power within the Americas—and in turn enabled the acts of literary and economic transmission inspiriting his own Cuban story." Brickhouse, *Transamerican*, 152–53.
36. Pérez, *Slaves*, 107.
37. Pérez, *Slaves*, 121, 125.
38. Scott, *Slave Emancipation in Cuba*, 13.
39. Scott, *Slave Emancipation in Cuba*, 14.
40. Pérez, *Slaves*, 114.

then in the United States concerning the annexation of Cuba to our confederacy; you may be curious, perhaps, to know what they say of it here" (193). In expounding on this idea, Bryant goes on to quote not a Cuban but a "European who had long resided in the island." According to his source, "The Creoles [. . .] would be very glad to see Cuba annexed to the United States, many of them ardently desire it," mainly because it would "open their commerce to the world, rid them of a tyrannical government, and allow them to manage their own affairs in their own way" (193). However, this European notes that Spain will never give up Cuba, and that neither "will the people of Cuba make any effort to emancipate themselves in taking up arms" (193). The unnamed source does add that it would be dangerous for any Cuban planter to speak in favor of annexation to the United States since they "would run the risk of being imprisoned or exiled" (193). While this European erroneously predicts that Cubans would not fight for their own independence from Spain, he acknowledges that they cannot even mention the word subversion because Spanish repression would be severe, matter-of-factly naturalizing the brutal political suppression that Cubans suffered under Spain. Still, Bryant's account suggests that the Cubans simply do not have it in them to free themselves, again underscoring their inferiority.

Bryant concludes his account by linking Cuba to the United States in a cautionary way, noting that while the annexation would be positive for the island it would be less so for the larger nation. Bryant states:

> Negroes would be imported in large numbers from the United States, and planters would emigrate with them. Institutions of education would be introduced, commerce and religion would both be made free, and the character of the islanders would be elevated by the responsibilities which a free government would throw upon them. (194)

Bryant suggests that the influx of US slaves and planters into Cuba would result in democratizing the island's government and culture so that Cubans would be improved through contact with US values. However, Bryant also examines the flip side, or the influence of Cuba on the United States, noting: "The planters [. . .] would doubtless adopt regulations insuring the perpetuity of slavery" (194). Bryant sees Cuba as negatively influencing the United States because it would enable proponents of slavery to secure its permanence, at the same time that the legal rights allowed by Spain to slaves in Cuba would be eliminated under US annexation. In this way, Bryant suggests that acquiring Cuba would make the United States a worse enslaver than it already was because the more inhumane traits of its planter class would be imposed on the island. Annexing Cuba, Bryant suggests, would amplify the geoculture of slavery operating in the US South, making it even more pernicious.

At the same time that Bryant racializes Cubans and sets them in opposition to himself and to other "strangers to the island," it is ultimately Cuba's perceived ability to bring out the worst in the United States that most concerns him, persuading him against advocating for annexation. The representations that he develops in his account set up Cuba as a place of negative influence, in both physical and moral terms, a location where women and men are more interested in artifice than in substance, and where spectacularized behavior estranges the observer from what is moral and true. Thereby, Bryant establishes Cuba not only as an inheritor of the "Black Legend" but also as a corruptive gothicscape where the troubling overlaps of race, gender, and nationality set the tone for how Cuba becomes gothicized in nineteenth-century transamerican narratives.

Similar to Bryant, Willis does not see annexation as a positive, but, differently, this is mostly because he does not see Cuba as ready for improvement. In addressing the annexation of Cuba as a given, Willis (anticipating the US invasion of Cuba in 1898) states:

> We are to see, probably, whether [Cuban culture] will stand the infusion of the blood, which, of all on earth is the most unlike it—the restless, hurried, scrambling, undignified-ly successful Yankee, and I hope Cuba will not be over-filibustered, but will remain so far Spanish, for the next fifty years, as to give a fair chance to the experiment. (280)

In this passage, Willis sets up US culture as the most globally in opposition to Cuba's, and notes how the dignity of the Cubans is not necessarily a positive trait juxtaposed to the undignified "Yankee." Further, by hoping that Cuba will not be invaded to achieve its de facto acquisition, Willis foreshadows a kind of imperialist nostalgia that wishes Cuba to remain a clear antithesis to what he has represented negatively as "Spanish," and the United States.[41] To that end, Willis—like Bryant before him—portrays Cuba as corruptive, a gothicscape in which people are performative, superficial, racialized, and inherently marred both by their connection to Spain and by the geoculture of slavery.

In keeping with the discourses of transamericanity disseminated by European and US travel writers, Bryant and Willis focalized their attention on and sexualized Cuban bodies, elaborating a gothicscape characterized by racialized performance and gendered spectacle. In her discussion of the representation of Caribbean sexualities as transgressive, Rosamond S. King argues that while the "Caribbean body has consistently been exploited for its labor," Caribbean peoples' "sexual behaviors have been derogated, exaggerated, and exoticized by imperial and colonial powers and then held up by those same powers as examples of Caribbean people's inferiority and as justification for their oppression."[42] Turning bodies into "sites of power," Bryant and Willis counterpoised Cuban women to US white women and Cuban (or "Spanish") men against Anglo-Americans.[43] Further, they set themselves as the racial/cultural standard, thereby subalternizing Cubans within the larger discursive frames of transamericanity.

By figuring the island as dangerous and corruptive, these two writers created a representational continuum articulated through the structures of a gothicscape. Both of these narratives establish the clear differentiation, and superiority, of the US "stranger" in the Cuban space, especially vis-à-vis the Cuban people. In focusing on what they found to be the island's troubling features, moreover, Bryant and Willis's Cuba travelogues do not simply enact the "imperial" gaze that Pratt has identified in similar travel narratives. While their critical gaze does take discursive possession of Cuba, they also both suggest that Cuba should not be acquired by the United States for the good of the larger nation. Unlike many of the Cuba guides identified by Pérez and Lazo,

---

41. Rosaldo has used the term "imperialist nostalgia" to describe the way that "agents of colonialism [. . .] often display nostalgia for the colonized culture as it was 'traditionally' (that is, when they first encountered it). The peculiarity of their yearning, of course, is that agents of colonialism long for the very forms of life they intentionally altered or destroyed." Rosaldo, "Imperialist Nostalgia," 107–08.

42. King, *Island Bodies*, 1.

43. King, *Island Bodies*, 18.

these two narratives craft gothicized representations of the island that not only draw on the "Black Legend" (anticipating how these figurations were used much more widely by the century's end), but also weld the geoculture of slavery onto the Cuban landscape and people. In fashioning Cuba as a corruptive gothicscape, Bryant and Willis's narratives are among the first to articulate some of the gothicized simultaneities that are further developed, disseminated, and challenged by the other writers in this study during the nineteenth century.

CHAPTER TWO

Gothicized Souths

Martin R. Delany's *Blake, or the Huts of America* and Louisa May Alcott's "Pauline's Passion and Punishment"

MARTIN ROBINSON DELANY (1812–1885) and Louisa May Alcott (1832–1888) were impassioned abolitionists who crafted gothicized representations of Cuba, specifically of its potential influence on the United States, before and during the US Civil War. Delany's novel, *Blake, or the Huts of America,* was partially serialized in 1859 and then published in 1862, and Alcott published "Pauline's Passion and Punishment" in 1862, winning a large financial prize for the story. Both of these texts belong to the group of nineteenth-century literary works that represented Cuba as a gothic geoculture. What sets these narratives apart is that these two writers, who never visited the island, wrote uncannily similar fictionalized stories that followed along the gothicized lines already drawn by other writers who had traveled to Cuba. In that context, this chapter focuses on how these narratives further gothicized Cuba by crafting what I call the *gothicized souths,* or the nineteenth-century literary constructs that represented the hemispheric region in gothic terms as demarcated and defined by the geoculture of slavery.[1] This figuration established a representational equation between the US

---

1. See my discussion of the "transamerican souths" in García, "Gothic Cuba and the Trans-American South." See also Anderson, Hagood, and Turner's *Undead Souths,* which includes works "spanning the collection of spaces and places identified

South and Cuba, which drew its persuasive power from signifying gender, race, and nation as imbricated markers of a corrupted and corruptive identity, especially for US white women.[2]

Within transamericanity, slavery functioned as a geoculture that produced and disseminated notions of a cultural continuum whose influence transcended local, regional, and even national borders. I focus here on how, in contributing to the representational spectrum of nineteenth-century gothicized figurations of Cuba, Delany and Alcott drew principally on the trope of doubleness—of the gothic or negative double—to articulate the potentially dangerous relationship between the United States and Cuba.[3] In doing so, they both created protagonists who embodied doubleness in troubling ways. Delany did so by suggesting that his hero Blake's doubleness—his familiarity with both Cuban and US cultures—made him more effective in his mission to ignite a hemispheric slave revolt. Alcott used the trope of duality to show how exposure to Cuba transforms her heroine, Pauline, into the narrative's gothic monster by setting in motion the tragic denouement—including the death of her Cuban husband—undeterred by the compunctions of her better self. These gothicizations articulate and exploit extant anxieties about a rising US empire and its relationship to Cuba during this time.

Recent scholarship has explored the connections between the US South and the hemisphere. In discussing "the hemispherics of the mid-century South," Matthew Pratt Guterl has described the region "as a borderlands between the North American republic, the Caribbean, and Latin America," categorizing this area as "an American Mediterranean" (98). He has further argued for conceiving hemispherically of "a fraternity of slaveholders," who were "connected—by ship, by overland travel, by print culture, by a sense of singular space, and by the prospect of future conquests—to the *habitus* and *communitas* of New World slaveholders, to institutions, cultures, and 'structures of feeling' that were not contained by the nation-state."[4] In relation to the gothic, Susan Castillo Street and Charles L. Crow note how the US South "is

---

as southern from the Appalachians southward to the Caribbean and stretching into the U.S. West." Anderson, Hagood, Turner, *Undead Souths*, 3.

    2. García, "Gothic Cuba," 161.

    3. For a history of the Gothic double, see *The Encyclopedia of the Gothic*, 189–95.

    4. Guterl, *American Mediterranean*, 1.

a region that has always been obsessed with crossroads and boundaries, whether territorial (the Mason-Dixon line) or those related to gender, social class, sexuality and particularly race."[5] Along those lines, Edward Sugden has theorized a "Gothic South," globalized in the nineteenth century "as a network of colonial inheritances as well as continuing transnational overlaps" through "a mixture of the colonial, the conceptual, and the material."[6] Gretchen J. Woertendyke has argued for the "hemispheric regionalism" of the romance within "all regions touched by the slave trade" in the Americas, advocating for its recognition "as a future-oriented form, one in which the competing strains of imperial expansion and xenophobic retraction, combine." Specifically in relation to the gothic romance, Woertendyke observes how the fear of slave insurrection—symbolized by the former French colony of Saint Domingue—"became a specter of possibility and horror across the Atlantic world."[7] The literary regionalization that joined the gothic to the US South, Cuba, and Latin America was itself comprised of an implicit duality—based on what Woertendyke identifies as the tension between empire and xenophobia—that this chapter focuses on.

Against the backdrop of this slave-based commonality, Rodrigo Lazo has noted how words such as "strange" and "exotic," which were used to describe Cuba, emphasize "the relativity of viewpoint in travel pieces, which were usually written by upper-class travelers and writers from New England."[8] This relativity—this setting of Cuba in opposition to the United States—became even more common between the 1840s and 1850s, when US imperialist interest in Cuba reached its apex, and also when "a cadre of Cuban exiles" settled in the United States.[9] Anna Brickhouse notes how this tradition of transamerican "human and literary traversals" inspired Delany to address the "cultural and political crossings between Cuba and the United States" in his novel.[10] For Alcott, Susan S. Williams has argued, using Cuba as a stand-in for the US South suggested "that Southern indolence and its institution

---

5. Castillo Street and Crow, *Southern Gothic*, 2.
6. Sugden, "The Globalisation of the Gothic South," 74.
7. Woertendyke, *Hemispheric Regionalism*, 3, 22.
8. Lazo, *Writing to Cuba*, 9.
9. Lazo, *Writing to Cuba*, 2. He points to how during this time period, "presidents James Polk (1845–49), Franklin Pierce (1853–57), and James Buchanan (1857–61) all tried to purchase the island from Spain." Lazo, *Writing to Cuba*, 8–9.
10. Brickhouse, *Transamerican*, 152.

of slavery can infect the national body as a whole, stripping women of the discipline that makes them suitable mothers, writers, nurses, and healers of the nation."[11] As writers who never visited the island, but for whom this location had a specific signification, Delany and Alcott contribute to the gothicization of Cuba within nineteenth-century transamericanity.

By engaging with such representational patterns, Delany and Alcott also showed how they were steeped in a literary tradition that had long contrasted Cuba to the US South. In their many writings about Cuba, US Northerners routinely compared the two, including the abolitionist Julia Ward Howe, who in her 1860 travelogue remarks on the "indolence and mechanical ineptitude" of Cubans as a major obstacle to abolition.[12] She also notes the unlikelihood "that the men of our own far South will ever conceive as possible another social *status* than the present relations between master and slave."[13] Differentiating between Cuba's incompetence and the South's desire for power, Howe counterpoises discourses of Cuban inferiority against those of US exceptionalism. Even when the contrast was not this explicit, as Christopher Mark McBride has argued about Richard Henry Dana, Jr.'s 1859 writings on Cuba, the "racial elision" was part of "an ongoing trend [. . .] echoed by a number of his contemporaries in their Cuban travel narratives."[14] McBride adds that while "Dana was witnessing the parallel to slavery in the United States, [. . .] he chose not to lash out against this terrible situation," reflecting the ways in which such critiques were limited "by the capitalist paradise that Cuba represents for influential American interests."[15] Whether explicit or implicit, the analogy between the island and the US South was a literary commonplace by the time Delany and Alcott chose to figure Cuba in their respective writings.

Drawing on the kinship they saw between the US South and Cuba because of their shared ties to slavery, Delany and Alcott gothicized the island in two main ways:

---

11. Williams, *Reclaiming Authorship*, 104.
12. Ward, *A Trip to Cuba*, 233.
13. Ward, *A Trip to Cuba*, 234.
14. McBride, *Colonizer Abroad*, 36.
15. McBride, *Colonizer Abroad*, 40.

- First, not only do both Delany and Alcott connect the US South and Cuba as links in a longer geocultural chain, often establishing the island as a double of the southern states, but they also represent Cuba as inherently more dangerous—as a kind of south of the South. In this way, Cuba is figured not only as geographically below the US South, but also as a cautionary example of what the United States might become if the geoculture of slavery was allowed to proliferate.
- Both writers also draw on the gothic trope of doubles, with Delany applying this narrative structure to his protagonist and hero, explicitly doubling Blake's identity as grounded in both Cuban and US cultures to enhance his dangerousness. Like Delany's hero, Pauline becomes her own double—even describing her own transformation after living in Cuba like that of being possessed by an evil spirit.

However, unlike Blake—whom Delany portrays as gaining strength and agency in his abolitionist cause from this duality—Pauline's doubleness ultimately makes her a tragic figure. In what is essentially a cautionary tale of a woman's self-destruction because she uses her sexual power for revenge, Alcott's narrative—a kind of gendered negative double to Delany's story—transforms Pauline into its gothic monster, enacting a morality play that is fundamentally about Cuba's noxious influence.

Delany, born in 1812 to a free mother and a slave father in what is now West Virginia, is considered the first nineteenth-century black nationalist and separatist because he broke with the more integrationist strategies of his contemporaries.[16] In the late 1840s, Delany worked with Frederick Douglass in co-editing the abolitionist newspaper *North Star* and published some of his most political essays about race and slavery in that paper.[17] Over the course of his seventy-two years, and through the many professions Delany was involved in—including essayist, physician, inventor, novelist, explorer, and infantry major during the US Civil War—his perspective significantly evolved.[18] In what Robert M. Kahn has called Delany's "life-long odyssey," the writer

---

16. Miller, "Introduction," xiii, xxv.
17. Chiles, "Within and Without Raced Nations," 338.
18. Kahn, "The Political Ideology of Martin Delany," 415.

traveled through the US Northeast, Midwest, and the South, as well as abroad to England, Canada, and Africa.[19] These national, regional, transnational, and transcultural experiences gave Delany what scholars have described as his "Pan-Africanist" and transnational viewpoints, which he vested in his novel's hero, Blake. Through Blake's representation, Delany disseminated a distinctly hemispheric perspective, one that contributed to delineating the borders of the gothicized souths I focus on here, which not only linked peoples of African descent throughout the Americas, but also promoted the cultural continuums that joined diverse geographies.[20]

Delany's novel, as Brickhouse has argued, "explores the political implications of transamerican literary transmission as well as various symbolic forms of translation."[21] Floyd J. Miller, who edited and published the novel in 1970, argues that Delany saw a "black Cuba" as eventually leading "to the downfall of slavery in the United States."[22] Within the novel's narrative structure, Blake's avowed purpose in traveling to Cuba is to rescue his wife, who is sold by her master to slave traders. However, his goal is also to fuel a mass slave rebellion on the island, one he hopes will, in turn, spur insurrection throughout the US South. In Delany's time, Blake's plan would have raised not only the specter of Haiti's slave-led revolution, but also, and more immediately for US readers, that of slave rebellions at home, such as Nat Turner's revolt in 1831 and John Brown's attack on Harpers Ferry in 1859. In extending his novel's action to Cuba, as Ifeoma C. K. Nwankwo has argued, "Delany elbows his way into the raging debate about the annexation of Cuba," supported by US proslavery forces and by many among the Cuban elite.[23] Delany thereby radically recasts the annexation debate, positioning the island as desirable not as a potential slave state, but as a trigger for abolition, a consequence he wanted his audience to understand as

---

19. Kahn, "The Political Ideology of Martin Delany," 415.
20. McGann, in his 2017 edition of Delany's novel, notes how in 1839 the writer "made an extended tour through the South to learn what he could about the social and political condition of black there" and how the "trip provided the materials" for several chapters in the novel. Thirty years later, Delany left the United States "for a year's stay in West Africa, where he made arrangements to found a community in the Niger Valley." McGann, "Introduction," x, xi.
21. Brickhouse, *Transamerican*, 127.
22. Miller, "Introduction," xxii.
23. Nwanko, "The Promises and Perils of African-American Hemispherism," 585.

preferable when juxtaposed to what he represented as the inevitable possibility of a violent—and hemisphere-wide—slave rebellion.

With that end in mind, Delany also draws on gothic elements to represent Cuba as a double of the larger nation-cum-empire, but he does so from a uniquely transamerican perspective that figures the island as an empowering influence on black characters. In addition to drawing on the gothic, because of its established relationship to history and slavery, Delany pledged what he described as a "commitment to verisimilitude" to bolster his political message. He sought to accomplish this through the "authenticating" footnotes he includes in the narrative, which are meant to underscore the factuality of some of the novel's most horrific depictions.[24] Andy Doolen notes that Delany, like some of his contemporaries, anticipated the work of twentieth-century postcolonial writers by mixing politics and history into his fiction.[25] He adds that Delany, along with other African American writers at the time, believed "that by transforming the production of knowledge, they could help topple the slavery regime."[26] Thus, Delany sought to craft a counternarrative to Harriet Beecher Stowe's *Uncle Tom's Cabin* by drawing on factual sources for his gothic representations as a means to persuade readers that a slave rebellion was not only a fear of the past, but also actually unavoidable in the future. Further, he cast this threat not only as US-centered but as one that would have explosive hemispheric proportions and consequences.

In Delany's novel, this hemispheric perspective is evident through his focus on the "white paranoia," as Rebecca Skidmore Biggio has termed it, shared by Cuban and US slaveholders. While Delany is not reticent when describing horrific scenes of torture endured by slaves, the novel deploys its most fearsome overtones in its description of this "apprehension" that white slave owners lived with, within the context of these gothicized souths. Biggio argues that in the novel the slaves are "never paranoid" because a constant state of watchfulness and alarm was routine among enslaved blacks. Within the narrative, therefore, and "because they already know the worst, fear of the unknown has virtually no power over slaves, while it is crippling for

---

24. Doolen, "Be Cautious," 155.
25. Doolen, "Be Cautious," 154.
26. Doolen, "Be Cautious," 154.

most slaveholders."[27] In adding to existing scholarly work on Delany's novel, I focus here on less explored gothic aspects, which seem especially aimed at an intended white audience. In gothicizing parts of his only work of fiction, Delany targets those readers who might have failed to realize what he describes toward the novel's end as the "powder bin" inhabited by white slave owners, which would affect anyone who benefited from slavery. By representing the institution of slavery through a gothicized lens, Delany held up a narrative mirror for his white readers—both in the North and South—in which they could find reflected not only their own fears of slave revolts, but also how they were implicated within the hemispheric geoculture of slavery and how it corrupted them as a people and as a nation.

By aiming the gothicized aspects of his narrative at a white audience, Delany focuses parts of the novel's Cuba section on the corruptive influence of slavery on white women. Near the end of the novel, just before the slave insurrection is set in motion, the narrator tells how the wife of a planter in Cuba has a nightmare that largely foretells the revolt Blake is secretly orchestrating. A "bearer of despatches" from a delegation of landowners in Matanzas seeks a meeting with the Spanish Captain General to tell him that

> some thirty miles in the interior from Matanzas, the wife of a respectable planter had doubtless from impressions made upon her mind by the reality, become a maniac, making the most startling disclosures. An insurrection was to be commenced on their own plantation, she having been a party to the scheme. Talking incessantly, she raved and screamed, frequently startled, calling for a black chief to protect her. (297)

The beginning of this lengthy passage establishes a link between slavery and madness through the wife of the slave owner. This mental imbalance has led the woman to foretell the revolt and to implicate herself in the plan, underscoring the vulnerability of white women within the geoculture of slavery. As a result, the nameless woman talks "incessantly," demanding attention to her ravings. Moreover, she rejects her husband's and the Spanish military's protection, calling instead for a

---

27. Biggio, "The Specter of Conspiracy," 450.

"black chief" to save her, demasculinizing the white men and raising the specter of miscegenation.

The gothicized passage further builds on the fear of black male power over white women when the narrator describes how, in order to "dispel the phantom" and appease the raving woman, a slave child was placed on her bed, "with the assurance that it was the child of the Negro chief sent in advance of him" (297). This quiets the wife, but not before the narrator focalizes the reader's attention on the woman to explain her dream: "She had imagined herself in a horrible seclusion or cave surrounded by black serpents, when being attacked by a huge monstrous serpent, was only protected from certain death by the timely interposition of one of those divine black spirits" (297). The white woman sees herself trapped and endangered by slavery, held in a claustrophobic space at the mercy of "black serpents" bent on her destruction, especially the one "monstrous" snake. Perhaps more disturbing for Delany's intended white readership, this woman "mothers" the child of the black "chief," implying an interracial sexual relationship. Delany's purpose here is to draw on gothicized tropes to posit that white women are the most vulnerable victims of the geoculture of slavery in relation to Cuba.

Further, Delany uses this implicit vulnerability as a caution that imbues the white woman character in this scene with symbolic meaning, especially because she "raves" about the revolt that the reader knows is actually being planned by Blake. In making this representational choice, Delany not only imbricates race, gender, and nationality, but also once more places US characteristics in a superior position, just as he does with Blake. Unlike the Spaniards, the planters of Matanzas, whom Delany describes as "generally being Americans" (298), do not dismiss the woman's dream. Instead, the messenger tells the Captain General that the US planters want troops there as protection, and even ask the Spaniard to travel to the region to see for himself. When the Spanish governor asks what doctors have done to treat the woman, the messenger replies: "They can do nothing at all" (297), suggesting that Western medicine cannot restore the white woman to her senses. That the US slave owners in Matanzas believe that the woman's ravings should be taken seriously suggests they are smarter than their Spanish counterparts, especially since they believe what the colonizing authorities dismiss as madness. By aligning the reader's own knowledge with that of the US planters, Delany draws on the same notion of US exceptionalism that makes Blake such an effective hero.

In the same way that the novel constructs Blake as the quintessential "American" hero because of his independence of mind and action, the reader knows that the US planters in Matanzas are right to fear the woman's premonition, and that the Spaniards are wrong. The narrator tells how the Captain General, "a proud and haughty Castilian," believes Americans to be "a restless, dissatisfied class, ever plotting schemes to keep up excitement in the island, thereby having continual cause for complaint," so he dismisses their concerns (298). The passage continues with the Spaniard rejecting the plea that he send troops to Matanzas, arguing that it would be pointless to pay attention to the woman's fears of "black ghosts," and notes "that it is neither the desire nor duty of the executive of this colony to carry the national troops in battle array to divert the phantoms of a prostrated maniac" (297). Because the reader knows that these are not mere "phantoms," the white woman here becomes a stand-in for Cuba herself, which is better understood by the US Americans than by the Spaniards who rule it. By dismissing the mere "phantoms" conjured by a "maniac," the Spanish ruler sounds the death knell for the whites on the island, and Delany invests this moment with gothicized dramatic irony while also establishing the US characters—as he has done with Blake—as more connected to Cuba than the Spanish colonizers.[28]

In addition to building the novel's gothicized structure on the fear of white women's corruption, Delany also represents Cuba as an uncanny gothic double of the United States. Eric J. Sundquist argues that Delany wanted "to accentuate the fact that the Cuban situation was a kind of twin, a shadow play, of the American South for masters and slaves alike."[29] But while Delany drew on a cultural commonplace that saw Cuba and the US South as conjoined by slavery, he did not simply portray the island as a stand-in for the US South. Instead, Delany implicated the North as an accomplice to and beneficiary of "the

---

28. Hendler has noted how "throughout the novel, black interpretive abilities are highlighted by their juxtaposition with white ignorance and persistent incomprehension." Hendler, *Public Sentiments*, 69. That Delany gives the US planters in this scene access to greater "interpretive abilities" than other whites in the novel makes their connection to Blake's exceptionalism more salient.

29. Sundquist, *To Wake the Nations*, 185.

crimes of southern slaveholding," representing the system of human enslavement as "the crux of U.S. society."[30] The novel's gothic "shadow play" purposefully connects Cuban and US slaveholders to craft a cautionary tale with a transamerican goal. Delany's aim was not solely to call attention to the corruptive nature of the South's slave-based economy, but to propose that it created a continuum of experience throughout the hemisphere—as part of these gothicized souths—through the geoculture of slavery.

Within this context, Delany builds the sense of fear in his novel by creating a hero whose influence is transamerican. Further, Blake embodies the triangulation of the United States, Africa, and Cuba, created by the Atlantic slave trade, so that slavery becomes the geocultural thread that fuses different valences into Blake's persona. For one, we find out that while the "pure black" Blake was originally raised in Cuba as "Carolus Henrico Blacus" (192), he was actually "African born" (200).[31] As Blake explains to his "cousin," whom Delany represents as the real-life Afro-Cuban poet Gabriel de la Concepción Valdés, known as Plácido, once Blake arrived in the United States he Anglicized himself "going by the name of Henry Blake" (192). Thus, the narrative blurs distinctions between US and Cuban slavery through Blake's multiple yet interconnected identities. Through this plot device, Blake becomes the ultimate double because he embodies his own doubleness. This is not only because he manifests the inherent hemispheric influence of slavery, but also because he perceives his identity as transamerican (in addition to transatlantic and Pan-African), choosing to identify as a kind of inchoate Cuban-American. But when Blake tells "Placido" that he is "the lost boy of Cuba" (192), the reader is surprised. That he identifies himself as Cuban is initially confusing, because he has been so clearly connected to the United States. This narrative disjunction, however, make sense within the gothic contours of the double. Blake's reconnection with his Blacus identity in Cuba gestures toward the empowering duality that makes him more dangerous as a leader within the novel's gothicized framework.[32]

---

30. Sundquist, *To Wake the Nations*, 190. Doolen, "Be Cautious," 157.
31. Miller, "Introduction," xxiii.
32. In comparing Delany's novel with Mary Peabody Mann's *Juanita*, which I discuss in chapter 3, Havard notes: "Delany emphasizes slavery's transnational nature, highlighting how the slave trade leveled the national boundaries Mann seeks to pro-

Because of his doubleness, Blake becomes an intermediary between the rebellion in the United States and the one in Cuba, a connection rhetorically designed by Delany to raise both hope and fear about the potential liberation of slaves by a Messiah-like leader. Blake first sows the seeds of rebellion in the US South, and then arrives in Cuba to tell "Placido" that he has done so with the purpose of helping "to free my race," remaking that he has already "done in another place" what he "desire[s] to do" in Cuba (195). In that way, Blake presents himself as an experienced revolutionary, one who has already set in motion a revolt stateside. In response, Delany's Placido says: "Heaven has, indeed, [. . .] decreed your advent here to—," ready to suggest that Blake is their savior. But Blake cuts him off to interject the phrase: "Learn from you!" In this exchange, Blake refuses Placido's deference, but Placido disagrees, stating: "No, but to teach us what we need" (197). Jerome McGann, who in 2017 published a "corrected edition" of the novel, argues that Delany's literary resurrection of Placido (who was actually executed in 1844 as a leader of a failed slave insurrection) is meant "to replay historical events that had occurred more than ten years before [. . .] in order to rethink their significance for the future of black liberation."[33] By hailing Blake as the expected deliverer of his enslaved people, Delany's Placido invests the novel's protagonist with a hemispheric power, albeit centered on his US identity.

Indeed, while Blake is African by birth and Cuban by acculturation, the narrative clearly grounds his efficacy as a revolutionary in his belief in US ideals of equality. In that way, Blake is presented as a perfected version of the Blacus he was born as—a free black man whose experience as a slave in the United States turns him into a revolutionary. That triangulation of his African roots, Cuban nurture, and US education occurs within the Blake-Blacus duality that Placido (as conceived by Delany) celebrates as what the rebel slaves in Cuba need to succeed in their quest for emancipation. That Delany assigns the role of liberator to his fictional Cuban-American hero, rather than to Placido (who was actually executed by the Spanish colonial government for conspiring in

---

tect. For Delany, the meaningful division is not that between nations but rather that between an international white commercial and slaveholding elite and an exploited black Atlantic underclass." Havard, "Mary Peabody Mann's *Juanita* and Martin R. Delany's *Blake*," 510.

33. McGann, "Introduction," xvii.

the cause of Cuban independence), firmly grounds the novel in ideals of US exceptionalism. Delany's Blake can draw on the elements associated with what made the United States exceptional, as opposed to his African or Cuban legacies, as his most effective weapons in the struggle for freedom.

In addition to suggesting that Blake's duality makes him more dangerous as a rebel leader, in the penultimate chapter of the novel the narrator more firmly articulates the connections between these gothicized souths by addressing the reader directly:

> Few people in the world lead such a life as the white inhabitants of Cuba, and those of the South now comprising the "Southern Confederacy of America." A dreamy existence of the most fearful apprehensions, of dread, horror and dismay; suspicion and distrust, jealousy and envy continually pervade the community; [. . .] A sleeping wake or waking sleep, a living death or tormented life is that of the Cuban and American slaveholder. For them there is no safety. A criminal in the midst of a powder bin with a red-hot pigot of iron in his hand, which he is compelled to hold and char the living flesh to save his life, or let it fall to relieve him from torture, and thereby incur instantaneous destruction, nor the inhabitants of a house on the brow of a volcano could exist in greater torment than these most unhappy people. (305)

Delany here associates the idea of fateful anticipation not with the slaves on the brink of the violent rebellion that his hero, Blake, is planning. Instead, the apprehension of destruction, narrated in gothicized terms of "horror and dismay," is focused on the white "criminals" whom Delany links through a geocultural context.

Through the notion of a shared "living death," promoted by the transamerican system that connected Cuban and US slave owners, Delany's novel fuels existing anxieties as a way to persuade readers about the urgency of abolishing slavery. Along these lines, Sundquist has argued that Delany creates "a fictive world in which Cuban and American slavery are yoked together in historical simultaneity."[34] This historicized foundation for Delany's novel—which was serialized

---

34. Sundquist, *To Wake the Nations*, 184.

alongside contemporary nonfiction articles and news in two African American journals—contributes to its gothic shadowings. Biggio has identified moments when Delany's fictionalized descriptions, which seem to be exaggerations, are actually embellishments of contemporary historical accounts.[35] In this way, Delany could argue that the geoculture of slavery made Cuba and the United States reflections of each other, simultaneously implicated in a hemispheric crime, part of the gothicized souths trapped in a proverbial "powder bin," ready to explode. Further, as McGann has argued, the interconnection between the gothic and factuality in the novel serves to demonstrate how "the terror in *Blake* is far more terrible because of its historical and geopolitical extent."[36]

Similar to Delany, Alcott drew on the gothic tropes of doubling and corruption in her first prize-winning short story, titled "Pauline's Passion and Punishment." Published under a pseudonym in 1862, the gothic romance tells a cautionary tale through the representation of its heroine, Pauline Valary. The story is among some one hundred extant narratives that Alcott wrote and published anonymously or pseudonymously in popular magazines and journals before becoming a literary celebrity for her second novel, *Little Women* (1868). Alcott sharply distinguished her sensational "blood & thunder" stories, as she termed them, from what she described as her "moral pap" for young readers.[37] In many of these tales, Alcott addressed topics that were social taboos, especially for white middle-class women in her time, including drug addiction, murder, and interracial love affairs.[38] But while Alcott made a living producing these stories of "blood, sex, and violence," she did not acknowledge them as her own while she lived.[39] These gothic romances were perceived to be culturally below—in terms of genre and taste—the adult novels and the children's fiction Alcott penned. She kept her authorship secret, even though she made her famous protagonist, Jo March, a successful writer of such stories in *Little Women*. But thanks to the work of literary sleuths Leona Rostenberg and Madeleine Stern, we now know the connection between Alcott and her melo-

---

35. Biggio, "The Specter of Conspiracy," 442.
36. McGann, "Introduction," xx.
37. Stern, *Critical Essays*, 8.
38. Stern, *Unmasked*, xxiv.
39. Doyle, *Louisa May Alcott and Charlotte Brontë*, xix.

dramatic, often gothicized, stories so that Alcott's initial reputation as the author of mostly didactic children's literature has been radically revised.[40]

Born in 1832, a year after the Nat Turner Rebellion had shaken the United States, Alcott was the second daughter of Bronson and May Alcott, or Abba, as her mother was more familiarly known. Within the context of US racial politics at the time, Sarah Elbert has pointed to a "cloudy but nevertheless intriguing racial enigma within the Alcott household," involving Louisa and her mother.[41] Elbert notes how the Mays may have been of Portuguese Jewish descent, which would explain why Louisa and her mother, both of whom had "considerable tempers and admittedly passionate natures," also had dark complexions.[42] In contrast, Bronson was blond and blue-eyed and "persisted in believing that Anglo-Saxon 'races' possessed more spiritually perfect natures, were generally 'harmonious,' and had more lofty intellects than darker-skinned people." Bronson often referred to his wife and daughter as his "two devils," noting that he was not yet "quite divine enough to vanquish the mother fiend and her daughter."[43] Bronson's gothicized descriptions of Abba and Louisa, and his notion that he represented an opposition to their "darker" natures, provide a sense not only of the racial tensions in Alcott's household, but of how her own self-conception was gothicized, especially in relation to race. Her father's vision of her may help explain why, before writing *Little Women*, Alcott penned so many "abolitionist interracial romances" that pushed back against

---

40. Doyle, *Louisa May Alcott and Charlotte Brontë*, xviii. Alcott's pseudonymous and anonymous identities function as "dark" doubles to her established authorial persona. Similar to Sophia Peabody, who repressed the persona she crafted in her letters from Cuba, which I examine in the next chapter (and who was Alcott's neighbor in Concord when the latter was just a girl), Alcott publicly concealed her authorship of most of her gothic tales. She also borrowed from the gothic and looked to Cuba in her first 1864 novel, *Moods*, to craft the character of a Cuban "villainess," Ottila, intent on corrupting the novel's US American hero, Adam Warwick, modeled after Henry Thoreau. Although Alcott later eliminated the "Cuba plot" from the 1882 edition of that novel, the two opposite modes of writing—one focused on gothic romances and the other on didactic literature—manifest Alcott's own authorial doubleness.
41. Elbert, *Louisa May Alcott on Race, Sex, and Slavery*, xv.
42. Elbert, *Louisa May Alcott on Race, Sex, and Slavery*, xv.
43. Elbert, *Louisa May Alcott on Race, Sex, and Slavery*, xv–xvi.

social conventions at the same time as they challenged the racial hierarchy she had learned from her father.[44]

Stern has argued that this opposition, between the kind of story Alcott preferred to write and the type of novel she had to compose to retain literary fame and financial security, reflected a rift within the writer's own persona. Stern notes that as a child Alcott would "combine the threads of her own experience with the threads of the books she had read and interweave them into a fabric of her own creating."[45] Basing her analysis on Stern's assertion that Alcott's stories served her as a kind of "psychological catharsis," Miriam López-Rodríguez suggests that Alcott's choice of the gothic thriller, one of the most popular genres in her time, was motivated by the stress "accumulated in years of being told she was not the woman her father and patriarchal society expected her to be."[46] Whether the stories arose from recollections of her own personal trauma, and/or because she chafed against patriarchal expectations—societal and familial—Alcott's sensational stories "reveal an imagination that strays far from the expectations of middle-class domesticity."[47] Alcott was a nonconformist at heart, and most of her writings, from her adult stories to her literature for young readers, provide evidence of her feminist sensibilities and of her commitment to social change, both in women's rights and in the cause for abolition.

López-Rodríguez suggests that Alcott's initial choice of the gothic was also "in itself a political statement" because she was able to craft female characters who defied societal conventions. She adds that the element of having women "taking justice into their own hands" constitutes Alcott's "main innovative contribution to the Gothic short story."[48] In a genre in which heroines tended to be passive objects acted upon by heroes and villains, Alcott altered the formula so that the victimized ingénue turned into a dangerous femme fatale. Alcott's heroines invariably "know what they want and how to get it regardless of social conventions."[49] Though Alcott undoubtedly broke ground in the gothic thriller genre by crafting assertive women protagonists, in "Pauline's

---

44. Elbert *Louisa May Alcott on Race, Sex, and Slavery*, x.
45. Stern, *Behind a Mask*, xiii.
46. López-Rodríguez, "The Short Story as Feminist Forum," 39.
47. Elbert, *Moods*, xiii.
48. López-Rodríguez, "The Short Story as Feminist Forum," 39, 41.
49. López-Rodríguez, "The Short Story as Feminist Forum," 41.

Passion and Punishment," within the context of an expanding empire, the gender politics of a patriarchal system produce a duality in the protagonist that ultimately reinstates, rather than challenges, restrictions.

First published anonymously in Frank Leslie's *Illustrated Newspaper*, which specialized in sensational fiction, "Pauline's Passion and Punishment" earned Alcott her first major cash prize in a contest for the best short story, and cemented her mostly secret career as a writer of gothic thrillers. The story, initially set on a Cuban coffee plantation, introduces us to Pauline, a woman who has come to reduced circumstances and makes a living by working as a companion to a rich young girl.[50] Alcott's protagonist and gothic heroine, Pauline Valary, is described early in the story as having been "perfect" when she arrived in Cuba, but then becomes possessed by an "evil spirit" that Cubanizes (my term) her, "darkening" her both physically and morally. While in Cuba, Pauline becomes embroiled in a love affair with Gilbert, who has promised to marry her, but who jilts her in a letter after he decides to return to the United States to marry a wealthy heiress. Like Delany before her, Alcott crafts Cuba as a location where both geography and culture have an impact on the characters. In keeping with the discursive structures of transamericanity, Alcott describes Pauline as altered by the Cuban geoculture in ways that blur the racial and national lines that had initially separated her from Manuel Laroche, the young heir to the plantation, who is in love with her.

In an early scene in which the binary opposition between North and South is racialized, Pauline looks out of the windows, and though

---

50. This is one of the elements in Alcott's treatment of Cuba that suggest she may have been influenced not only by her own experiences as a companion (one of the occupations she pursued to make money for her family), but also by the experiences of Sophia Peabody, who had been her neighbor in Concord. Specifically, Sophia and her sister, Mary, whose texts I examine in chapter 3, traveled to a Cuban coffee plantation in the 1830s where Mary worked as a governess and where they lived for eighteen months. Although Mary and Sophia wrote about the slaves on the coffee plantation, there is no mention of slaves in Alcott's fictionalized plantation. Instead, the word "slavery" is used repeatedly by the characters—white and non-white—to describe psychological states, more specifically, Pauline's decision to seek revenge on her former fiancé. While there are no actual slaves in Alcott's story, the text is deeply concerned with the psychological repercussions of bondage for the human soul, especially the souls of US white women. In this way, Alcott appropriates the language of slavery—as many white feminists did in the nineteenth century—to call attention to the asymmetrical gender relations that "enslaved" white women.

she feels wooed by the sounds of "a Spanish contradanza," the narrator explains how, within this "southern scene," hers is

> not a southern face that looked upon it with such unerring glance; there was no southern languor in the figure, stately and erect; no southern swarthiness on fairest cheek and arm; no southern darkness in the shadowy gold of the neglected hair; the light frost of northern snows lurked in the features, delicately cut, yet vividly alive, betraying a temperament ardent, dominant, and subtle for passion burned in the deep eyes, changing their violet to black. (109)

The repeated word "southern" here conflates Cuba with the US South, turning them into doubles of each other. Further, the implied gothicized souths are clearly set in opposition not only to Pauline's superior abilities (her "unerring" look and her "stately" posture), but also to her sharply racialized body ("gold" hair and "fairest" skin on face and limbs). Williams has argued that within the story's "political allegory," Cuba is represented "less as a tropical paradise than as a potential slave state" so that we are to understand Pauline's alteration as one produced by being exposed to what is "southern" (101). The articulation that "languor," "swarthiness," and "darkness" define the southern character helps support Alcott's point that Cuba may be even worse than the US South in that it anticipates what the South might become if slavery is left unchecked.[51]

Even though Pauline is initially represented as being the opposite of what is "southern," the passion for revenge that she develops while in Cuba causes her to mutate, even altering her eyes from a royal "violet" to a racialized "black." Alcott first describes Pauline as a "handsome woman," pacing to and fro in her room, "like a wild creature in its cage," in the wake of a "mental storm, swift and sudden as a tempest of the tropics, [which] had swept over her and left its marks behind" (107). Through an inability to control her temper—considered a major flaw for women in Alcott's time (and something for which Alcott herself was often criticized by her father)—Pauline becomes infected by Cuba's geoculture, transforming into a caged wild animal. Although

---

51. Through the crafting of her Cuban female characters, Bannett notes, Alcott not only wished to craft a "political commentary on Cuban annexation" but also sought to reassert her "antislavery stance." Bannett, "Cuban Femininity," 138.

Pauline's country of origin is not explicitly given, she is coded racially as "white" through her pale skin and blonde hair, and the narrator tells us that "in the spirited carriage of the head appeared the freedom of an intellect ripened under colder skies" (109). The adjectives that identify her character as audacious, independent, and daring mark her as a being a Northerner from the United States, and, thereby, a symbol of idealized US white womanhood.

As she metamorphoses into a gothicized heroine, however, Pauline is not only further coded in darker racialized terms (appearing to be white on the outside but "black" on the inside), but she also degrades as an emblem of US womanhood. After the mental and moral "storm" she suffers once she finds out Gilbert has deserted her, Pauline asks Manuel to marry her, even though she is older and penniless (112). Her change into a femme fatale, Williams has argued, would have been understood as "a woman's revenge through socially acceptable means (subterfuge, romance, and charm)" (101). But by having Pauline propose marriage to a man several years her junior, especially one coded as racially inferior, and one she is not in love with, Alcott gothicizes Pauline by also associating her behavior to several social taboos. Because Pauline is assertive and subverts traditional gender roles, López-Rodríguez argues that she is one of Alcott's most "radical female protagonists."[52] However, while Pauline is decidedly forward in her actions, we are not meant to take her as a role model, especially given that the story builds up to a tragic ending.

The trope of doubleness begins to develop as Pauline explains her revenge plan to Manuel, and the narrator notes how she is driven on by the "dark mood" that takes "possession of her" and stifles "the generous warnings of her better self" (113). The gothic trope of better and worse selves acting in opposition to each other is fused to demonic possession as Pauline admits that a "strange spirit rules me" (113). The love she had for Gilbert, she continues, is now "a pale ghost that will not rest" until her former fiancé has experienced "an hour as bitter as the last" (113). After Pauline speaks, the narrator focalizes on how she has corrupted Manuel, bringing out the worst in his character, explaining that "the savage element that lurks in southern blood leaped up in the boy's heart as he listened," and Pauline, aware that "she had roused the

---

52. López-Rodríguez, "The Short Story as Feminist Forum," 38.

sleeping devil [. . .] was glad to see it!" (113). In the measure that Pauline becomes "possessed," she exploits Manuel's essentialized violent and easily corruptible "southern" personality for her own purposes. The story thereby begins to build the gendered fears of corrupted US white womanhood conjured because of Pauline's exposure to Cuba's geoculture.

At the same time that Alcott infantilizes Manuel as "a boy" to signal his racialized inferiority, Pauline is both "blackened" and masculinized as she admits that though it is "weak, wicked, and unwomanly" of her, she will persist "as any Indian on a war trail" to inflict her revenge on Gilbert (114). By using the stereotype of a warring Indian, Alcott conflates Pauline's racialization in Cuba with transamerican gothic tropes, describing her negative transformation in terms that reference white fears of Indian attack and of "going native." Further, Alcott suggests that by losing her status as a white woman Pauline becomes a dangerously racialized "Other." Pauline's regression is not only coded in negative racial and gendered terms, but she also becomes like an "Indian," suggesting that she has taken on a "savage" identity. However, this imbrication of race and gender in Pauline's corruption is not enough in Alcott's representation of her evident downfall. Further, and like Delany's hero, whose doubling is also figured in transamerican terms, Alcott crafts Pauline's transformation as one fusing race, gender, and nationality by shape-shifting her into a Cubanized woman.

After showing us Pauline's moral and physical deterioration, and her corruptive impact on Manuel, Alcott further raises the specter of racial mixing (or what was termed as miscegenation in the nineteenth century) to heighten the gothic melodrama.[53] When Pauline tells Manuel that she wants the "fortune, rank, splendor, and power" that only he can give her, she notices that he is "longing to ask the natural question [. . .] but too generous to utter it" (114). The text here implies that Manuel wants to know what he will receive in return, which suggests a commercial exchange: she marries him for money, and he gets the woman he desires. However, Pauline tells Manuel that she will give him her loving friendship and her pledge never to sully his name but "can promise no more." To this, Manuel, "like a true child of the south"

---

53. Rosenthal points to how the term "did not appear until relatively late in the history of interracial sex, which suggests the power of words to ossify reality or to organize hatred into a neatly quasi-scientific phrase." Rosenthal, *Race Mixture*, 4.

begins to cry, but finally tells Pauline to take "all I have—fortune, name, and my poor self" (115). Manuel's weeping after Pauline basically informs him that she will not have sex with him further infantilizes him and cements Pauline's control within an inversion of gender roles. Alcott thereby rejects the traditional seduction narrative, instead showing how Cuban geoculture turns Pauline into a predator.

Once Pauline and Manuel marry and travel to the United States to find Gilbert and his rich wife, the metamorphosis that begins for Pauline in Cuba takes an even stranger twist as she becomes Cubanized not just behaviorally but also physically. At one point, the narrator tells how Pauline stretches out "a truly Spanish foot" to her husband with "an air of smiling coquetry he had never seen before" (118). Shelley Streeby has noted how Pauline, first "described as a distinctively northern-European type," begins to change "as she indulges her passions and carries out her revenge, which involves marrying the handsome, wealthy Manuel."[54] That her foot becomes somehow "Spanish" racializes Pauline within the discursive constructs of the "Black Legend," and her coquettish ways also show her transformation in cultural terms. Unlike Delany's hero, Blake, who embodies and is empowered by US cultural traits while in Cuba, Pauline's move away from the island becomes the catalyst for her fully gothicized Cubanization in physical and cultural ways.

By the time Pauline finally finds Gilbert and his wife, Babie, the reader has been given the sense that Pauline has shed her white "skin" to become something "dark" and unwholesome. As they meet, Pauline reminds Babie that they knew each other as schoolgirls in the United States, and when Babie introduces Gilbert to Pauline, he can only stand, dumbfounded, "with downcast eyes and agitated mien, suffering a year's remorse condensed into a moment" (121). Pauline, having the upper hand, tells Gilbert that his wife is mistaken because "Pauline Valary died three weeks ago, and Pauline Laroche rose from her ashes" (121). Similar to Delany's Blake, who is his own double in these gothicized souths, Pauline describes herself as having a double. This representation suggests that the original white Pauline is dead and has been replaced by her Spanish/Cuban gothic double, which invests Pauline—like Blake—with dangerousness.

---

54. Streeby, *American Sensations*, 35.

In the climactic scene, after the two couples hike up a mountain, Pauline and Gilbert arrive first at the spot where they are all to meet, and their conversation gives us a more nuanced sense of Pauline's corrupted duality. The narrator sets the ambient tone and foreshadows the ending by noting: "Behind them roared the waterfall swollen with autumn rains and hurrying to pour itself into the rocky basin that lay boiling below, there to leave its legacy of shattered trees, then to dash itself into a deeper chasm, soon to be haunted by a tragic legend" (147). The forewarning that this tragedy will become legendary—or a story that becomes part of cultural tradition—establishes the structure through which readers should understand the forthcoming events. As part of her revenge, Pauline planned for Gilbert to fall back in love with her so she could reject him, and as they find themselves alone, he declares his rekindled love for her. Further, he suggests that Manuel and Babie, whom he describes as "children," have fallen in love with each other, and asks her to "come out into the world with me to lead the life you were born to enjoy" (147). Pauline, who has long waited for this moment, has "every power under full control, every feature obedient to the art which had become a second nature" (147). This idea that Pauline's two natures have merged, the one that has pretended to love Gilbert with the one that seeks revenge upon him, suggests that the boundary between her true and her pretended selves has disappeared.

The gothic melodrama reaches its apex once Pauline rejects Gilbert, as she planned to do all along, and when he, in near desperation asks, "How will it end?" referring to their conflict, Pauline replies forebodingly: "As it began—in sorrow, shame and loss" (150). Here, Pauline suggests that the asymmetry between them has been corrected because her shame at being deceived by Gilbert back in Cuba is eliminated by him finding himself rejected by her. Pauline taunts Gilbert by revealing the details of the subterfuge she has played with Manuel, and Gilbert vows that he "will end this jest of yours in a more bitter earnest than you prophesied," promising that she will "have one man's blood upon your soul" (152). When he asks Pauline whether Manuel can be roused "to forget your commands and answer like a man," Manuel, who has by then also reached the top, answers "Yes!" The two men scuffle, and when Pauline tries to intercede, Manuel flings her behind him, slapping Gilbert across the face with her glove. The narrator then tells us that "the wild beast that lurks in every strong man's blood leaped up in Gilbert" as he pushes Manuel over the edge of the precipice. When Manuel falls, Gilbert hears "a heavy plunge into the black pool below [with] that thrill of horrible delight which comes to murderers alone" (152). But right after, another rushing sound is heard, another plunge, "and then two figures [stand] where four had been [. . .] appalled at the dread silence that made high noon more ghostly than the deepest night." The gothicized tone is heightened because Pauline and Gilbert realize that Babie has thrown herself behind Manuel, giving credence to Gilbert's notion that his wife was in love with Manuel. The story ends with the narrator noting that in "that moment of impotent horror, remorse, and woe, Pauline's long punishment began," especially given that, even worse than Gilbert predicted, she has caused Manuel *and* Babie's deaths (152). Pauline's desire for revenge, therefore, is doubled and equalized both as her "passion"—the cause—and her "punishment"—the effect.

In my reading of Alcott's story, Pauline's doubleness is ultimately cautionary, especially as her change is explained largely in terms of possession by or enslavement to an evil spirit. By ending at the moment of Pauline's horrific realization, the story does not appear to offer a "forgiving image" of Pauline Laroche, as López-Rodríguez has suggested.[55] Instead, Alcott's story shows us that in becoming Pauline Laroche, Pauline Valary not only lost her better self but also suffered a bodily mutation that "darkened" her in dangerous and destructive ways. Her initial personal attributes and work ethic are so altered after her time in Cuba that Pauline is twice described in the story as laying about "indolently," and even her national affiliation appears to change when she refers to Cuba as her "home" (132, 136). By transforming herself into both a "warring Indian" and a Cubanized femme fatale, Pauline is represented as irremediably corrupted by Cuba's geoculture.[56] As Nina Bannett has argued, this threatening "Cuban woman was not merely an abstract being [. . .] but in fact, a living, breathing locus of national anxiety."[57] In crafting her anti-heroines as Cuban or Cubanized, Alcott

---

55. López-Rodríguez, "The Short Story as Feminist Forum," 39.
56. Rodríguez has argued that Pauline, like Ottila in Alcott's initial edition of her first novel, *Moods*, represents, within "the literary imagination of the nineteenth century United States [. . .] new versions of the 'tameless' and 'passionate' Caribbean woman always menacingly present in a world ordered by white, male, northern superiority." Rodríguez, "That mixture," 132.
57. Bannett, "Cuban Femininity," 159–60.

participated in the larger representational spectrum of texts produced within the context of nineteenth-century US imperialist expansion.

Delany and Alcott contributed to representing Cuba as a gothic geoculture by connecting Cuba—a place they had only visited in their imagination—to the US South as part of a larger continuum of gothicized souths. The dangerous duality inherent to and produced by this simultaneity is tinged with the gothic hues that empower Delany's Blake but destroy Alcott's heroine. Indeed, while Blake's "Americanization" becomes his strength in Delany's narrative, in which the hero embodies US ideals of exceptionalism, Pauline's increasingly powerful sexuality Cubanizes her and disconnects her from ideals of white "northern" womanhood. In reflecting an essentialized imbrication of gender, race, and nation within the Cuban geoculture, these narratives show how this overlap empowers Blake, as a black man, but dooms Pauline, as a white woman. That these works, inspired by Delany and Alcott's shared abolitionist stance, figured Cuba in similarly gothic terms reflects the representational simultaneities of the island's dangerousness that flowed through the gothicized souths of transamericanity.

CHAPTER THREE

Transgressive Hauntings

Sophia Peabody's *Cuba Journal* and
Mary Peabody Mann's *Juanita: A Romance
of Real Life in Cuba Fifty Years Ago*

IN ONE OF the last letters she wrote home from Cuba, near the end of her stay on the island, Sophia Peabody (who years later married Nathaniel Hawthorne) gothicized the creative and literary fervor she experienced there in terms of madness and demonic possession. Throughout the last volume of the *Cuba Journal*, as the almost nine-hundred-page, home-bound manuscript is known, both Sophia and her middle sister, Mary (who traveled to Cuba to work as a governess, bringing Sophia along as her sickly companion), represented her youngest sister's letter writing as maniacal. In that final letter, Sophia states that her experience in Cuba has caused a "trance-like" state in her (572), while Mary notes that her sister is "possessed with a writing demon the first thing in the morning" (575). Indeed, Sophia's compulsion to write "first thing" leads Mary to add, in an appendix to the letter dated January 21, 1835, "If I don't find an old stump of a pen in the chair some day instead of Sophia Peabody I will not say a *word* but really I sometimes feel concerned" (575, emphasis in original). Mary's qualification of "sometimes" feeling concerned is an understatement since she continually expressed profound worry over Sophia's behavior in Cuba. However, it is also particularly telling because Mary suggests that she expects Sophia's passion for writing to consume her, just as it consumes her writing implements. This gothicized preoccupation, that Sophia as writer would be extinguished by her passion for writing, is one of the hauntings we find in the relationship between the sisters as a result of their stay in Cuba.

While in their twenties, Sophia Amelia Peabody and Mary Tyler Peabody, daughters of a prominent Salem family, spent eighteen months in Cuba from December 1833 to May 1835. While on the island, Mary worked as a governess to the children of a coffee plantation owner and Sophia sought a "rest cure" for the disabling headaches that had plagued her for most of her life.[1] Sophia's highly literary letters, detailing her life in Cuba, were bound and hand-sewn by their older sister, Elizabeth, into the three volumes we know today as the *Cuba Journal*. This quasi-public work circulated widely among and beyond family and friends of the Peabodys during the sisters' time in Cuba, and for at least two decades after they returned to New England.[2] The diary-like letters are filled with intimate details, which Sophia's biographer, Patricia Dunlavy Valenti argues "obliterates the boundary between the reader and the subject."[3] These letters were also a main source nearly fifty years later for Mary's own antislavery novel, *Juanita: A Romance of Real Life in Cuba Fifty Years Ago*, published posthumously in 1887.

Locating Sophia's Cuba writings within the transamerican literary byways that connected the hemisphere through slavery, and within "the tangled genealogies of [US] and Cuban political and literary history," Anna Brickhouse notes that Sophia "experienced firsthand the interlocked nature of Cuban-[US] slaveholding interests."[4] Further, Sophia's experiences in Cuba were influential on Hawthorne, who read the *Cuba Journal* before meeting and later marrying Sophia, and quoted "more than sixteen passages from [the letters] into his first American Notebook."[5] In addition, Brickhouse remarks on how, many years later, "Hawthorne's interest in his wife's letters prompted her sister Mary Peabody to suggest that he write a novel of slavery and Cuban plantation life based on the journal—a fictional challenge he chose never

---

1. Valenti, *Sophia Peabody Vol. 1*, 52.
2. Valenti, *Sophia Peabody Vol.1*, 84.
3. Valenti, *Sophia Peabody Vol. 1*, 84.
4. Brickhouse, *Transamerican*, 26.
5. Badaracco, "Introduction," xviii.

to undertake."⁶ Locating the sisters's writings "among dozens of nineteenth-century books and articles about Cuba" predominantly produced by New England writers, Rodrigo Lazo also identifies Sophia's *Cuba Journal* as "a prime example of the cultural-economic connections that took travelers and invalids to Cuba."⁷ Like many New Englanders before and after, Sophia and Mary perceived Cuba as a means to attain personal benefit—Mary through a much-needed job and Sophia through the island's purportedly beneficent climate. Instead, Sophia and Mary's narratives stand out among the many nineteenth-century stories of Cuba because their exposure to the geoculture of slavery became a lifelong haunting that transcended both personal and literary borders.

Although both the journal and the novel share similarly gothicized representations, the sisters's narratives articulate an oppositional duality through their sharply divergent ways of figuring Cuba. Whereas Sophia welcomed, even relished, the sensual empowerment she felt while on the island, Mary abhorred nearly everything she experienced there. Indeed, as I discuss later in this chapter, Mary crafted her novelized cautionary tale by fictionalizing many of the personal experiences Sophia described in the *Cuba Journal*. In this way, the sisters and their texts function as negative doubles of each other in that they often articulate diametrically opposed interpretations of a shared experience. While in Cuba, Sophia described New England culture are repressive, a force that had kept her in a state of living death for most of her life. In contrast, she was electrified and emboldened—creatively and sensually—by the beauty of the lush tropical landscape around her, and by the stimulating social life she found among Cuba's slaveholding elite.⁸ In sharp opposition, Mary's Cuba was a hellish, slavery-infested gothicscape, where white, US-educated women were corrupted, and where the "superior" center of US cultural and political ideologies could not hold. Juxtaposing the *Cuba Journal* and *Juanita* reveals them to be texts not only haunted by Cuba's influence, but also how the first haunts

---

6. Brickhouse, *Transamerican*, 199.
7. Lazo, *Writing to Cuba*, 9.
8. Valenti's detailed study of the journal describes Sophia's need "to defend herself against charges of exaggeration and excessive enthusiasm." Valenti, *Sophia Peabody Vol. 1*, 55.

the other, adding important elements to the literary genealogy of the island's representations as a gothic geoculture within transamericanity.

Sophia's gothicization of her experience in Cuba, and the manner in which such gothic elements were later exploited by Mary in her novel, give these texts a salient place in this study. For one, Sophia's experiences in Cuba become what I call a *transgressive haunting*, both in her own letters and in her life, as well as in Mary's novel. Transgression, as scholars of the gothic have pointed out, "is a dominant quality of the [genre], and the status quo is always challenged" as boundaries collapse "between master/slave, self/other, insider/outsider, domestic/national, insular/global, colonial/imperial."[9] The notion of a transgressive haunting—based primarily on the fear of unleashed gendered constraints—adds to María del Pilar Blanco's idea of a "hemispheric haunting," one in which ghosts not only represent past memories, "but [also function] as commentaries on how subjects conceive present and evolving spaces and localities."[10] Along those lines, Cuba as a geoculture prompted behavior in Sophia that was perceived as transgressive by her and by others who categorized it as inappropriate and excessive, especially in relation to gendered expectations both in the United States and Cuba. I also draw here from Enrique Ajuria Ibarra's notion that "trauma and haunting meet at a crossroads where the ghost stands: it is a figure that brings the past into the present and feeds signification through its constant apparitions and [through] the [. . .] persistent enactment, emulation and stimulation of memory."[11] For the Peabody sisters, Cuba became a traumatic haunting, a ghostly place whose narrative representation in her letters haunted Sophia's sense of self, as well as her sister's fictionalized account of what they both witnessed and did while on the island.

These traumatic transgressions link Sophia and Mary's narratives to Blanco's notion that hemispheric hauntings, as narrative phenomena, are found within a context of US empire, "during a period when the Americas share a certain set of commonalities [through] simultaneous landscapes."[12] The geoculture of slavery in Cuba, repeatedly referenced in Sophia's journal and revisited as the main subject of Mary's

---

9. Elbert and Marshall, *Transnational Gothic*, 8.
10. Blanco, *Ghost-Watching American Modernity*, 6.
11. Ajuria-Ibarra, "Permanent Hauntings," 64.
12. Blanco, *Ghost-Watching American Modernity*, 6.

antislavery novel, contributes to what Blanco has identified as the "poetics of haunting" based on shared hemispheric "simultaneities."[13] Further, by adding a transgressive valuation to these poetics, Sophia and Mary contributed to the group of US writers whose stories represented geographies "in the process of being transformed, rather than simply describ[ing] locations where the past [was] interred."[14] Sophia and Mary's texts, however, are not only concerned with haunting as it relates to shared hemispheric landscapes such as slave plantations in Cuba and the US South. More importantly, they also repeat long-articulated anxieties of how the geoculture of slavery negatively transformed individuals exposed to its influence. This two-sided and future-looking anxiety—the joint concern over a possible haunting to come, not just over a haunting past, and over intimately personal, not just geographical, transmutations—is integral to how and why Sophia and Mary gothicized their narratives. In that way, these texts—on their own and in their relationship to each another—reveal the ways Cuba became a transgressive haunting within the discursive structures of nineteenth-century transamericanity.

For the purposes of my study, this chapter focuses on three main ways such hauntings operate within these narratives:

- First, Sophia's letters show how her own life choices in Cuba haunted her, specifically as they were gothicized by her and her sister, in addition to being represented as transgressive by herself and her family.
- Second, and nearly half a century later, Mary gothicized these concerns in Sophia's letters by fictionalizing them while also vesting two Cuban women characters who die in her novel with Sophia's own personal and artistic traits. To achieve this, Mary lifted parts of the *Cuba Journal* verbatim, something that suggests a clear rhetorical intent in signaling the dangerous, deadly cost of transgressive behavior.
- Finally, the major haunting in Mary's novel is her representation of Cuban slavery, which she embodies in one slave character, Camilla, who is gothicized as monstrous to symbolize the dangers of Cuba on the domestic space.

---

13. Blanco, *Ghost-Watching American Modernity*, 7.
14. Blanco, *Ghost-Watching American Modernity*, 16.

In representing the Cuban geoculture as pernicious, Mary manipulated her sister's narrative to her own ends. Here I trace the transgressive hauntings found within and between these texts—those that haunt Sophia's own sense of self by creating a gothicized dichotomy between her New England and Cuba personas, and those that later haunt Mary's fictionalized representation of women characters in her novel, who actually enact Sophia's own experiences. By doing so, we glean key aspects of how and why Cuba was gothicized during the nineteenth century as a geoculture that represented a peril for US white women.

Scholars have noted how, although Sophia's journal is not gothic in generic terms, it contains representations—of herself and of slavery—that give the *Cuba Journal* the gothicized penumbra this project focuses on. Diane Scholl has argued that slavery haunts and interrupts Sophia's journal, which is an otherwise largely buoyant narrative of female self-empowerment. Specifically, Scholl writes that in "describing the potential for renewed slave violence, as well as the history of insurrection that her [Cuban] hosts have witnessed or heard from survivors, Sophia's entries employ a keen element of Gothicism."[15] Scholl adds that Sophia, in describing the fear of slave revolts among her Cuban hosts, included "not only the bloodshed and horror of an uprising, but a sense of the dark, malevolent power dormant in the same slaves who grin and greet her so charmingly each morning."[16] In addition, and as I have previously noted elsewhere, Sophia identifies herself with transgressors, comparing herself to the biblical Eve, rewriting The Fall of Man in sexually suggestive terms, and extolling embodied representations of evil, such as Lucifer in Milton's *Paradise Lost*.[17] But at her most gothicized, Sophia describes herself, and is described by Mary, as being "possessed," thereby representing her transgressions not as an active choice on her part but as the influence of demonic forces implicitly conjured by Cuba's geoculture. In this way, Sophia abdicates responsibility for her actions, building on the representational constant of the island's corruptive influence.

Initially intended as private exchanges between Sophia and her mother, these letters from Cuba became extensively distributed among

---

15. Scholl, "Fallen Angels," 32.
16. Scholl, "Fallen Angels," 32.
17. For a discussion of her transgressive authorial persona, see García, "Transnational Crossings," 104.

the Peabodys's social and intellectual circle in Salem and Boston.[18] Though never formally published, the *Cuba Journal* became so well known that it gave Sophia a degree of literary fame, as the collected letters were read by many who were not part of the immediate family, including Hawthorne.[19] After returning to New England, she never allowed the *Cuba Journal* to be published, and even when she revisited the manuscript many years later, with the thought of editing it for publication, she ultimately decided against it.[20] In suppressing the journal, Sophia turned Cuba into a ghostly presence in her life, in keeping with her expressed discomfort at the letters being so broadly distributed among relatives, friends, and strangers.[21] In fact, Valenti has pointed out how, upon her return, Sophia rejected the way her self-representation in Cuba had been interpreted, and actively "sought to dissociate herself from the person she presented in the *Cuba Journal*."[22]

After she married Hawthorne, bore him children, and became his widow and editor, Sophia was still unwilling to have her Cuba writings printed. In 1869, when her first book, *Notes in England and Italy*, was published, the then-widowed Mrs. Hawthorne drew no connection between those travels with her husband and her first foray outside US borders as a traveling journalizer in Cuba.[23] Even further, when Sophia edited Hawthorne's American Notebooks for publication, she eliminated all the notes he had made from the *Cuba Journal*.[24] This reticence may have resulted from the fact that the collected letters, her first literary work, showed her in a light that did not conform to the image of "Mrs. Hawthorne" that she had so carefully constructed throughout her married life. The reserve Sophia showed toward the *Cuba Journal*, especially after becoming "Mrs. Hawthorne," is not surprising given the unrestrained exultation in her letters, which caused such concern to her mother, their main recipient, as well as to her sister, Mary.

---

18. Valenti, *Sophia Peabody Vol. 1*, 82.
19. Badaracco, "Introduction," xviii.
20. Hall, "Coming to Europe," 141.
21. Valenti, *Sophia Peabody Vol. 1*, 82.
22. Valenti, *Sophia Peabody Vol. 1*, 86.
23. For a comparison of Sophia's authorial persona in the *Cuba Journal* and her *Notes in England and Italy*, a compilation of the journals and letters from her and her husband's travels in Great Britain and Europe, see García, "Transnational Crossings."
24. Badaracco, "Introduction," xxci.

Both her mother and Mary repeatedly expressed their worries and, despite acknowledging them, Sophia continued to represent herself in transgressive ways, defying conventional expectations in her native New England and even in Cuba, developing a kind of split persona that Valenti has identified "as the dissonance between Sophia-in-Salem and Sophia-in-Cuba."[25] The chasm between how Sophia portrayed herself and how that representation was interpreted by her family led her to claim later that she had been coerced into the actions she described, or that these actions had been misrepresented.[26] Sophia's discomfort with how she was perceived, which appears to have contributed to her suppression of the *Cuba Journal,* not only haunts the text itself but creates a duality that is one of its major hauntings.

In the passage quoted above, Sophia's self-description of feeling hypnotized and Mary's comparison of her letter writing to a demonic possession point to how Sophia's creative productivity was perceived as troubling. For Mary, Sophia's obsession with producing her detailed journal-like letters conflicted with "the divine art of painting," which had brought Sophia some renown in New England but had no "chance of flourishing" as long as her sister "[wore] out her pens and tire[d] her fingers" (575). This representation sets Sophia's choice of artistic medium while in Cuba on the transgressive side of a binary opposition. Sophia was consumed by the desire to paint with words (as Valenti describes her writing), but Mary gothicized this need in oppositional terms between the divine and the demonic. Even more so, Mary suggested it was a diseased compulsion, which kept Sophia from her more proper and former vocation of painting. By devoting so much time to creating word paintings, Sophia transgressed the expectations that Mary (and everyone else in her family) had for her while in Cuba, a major theme that cuts across the *Cuba Journal* from beginning to end.[27]

In addition to the tropes of demonic possession and madness, there are two other main forms of transgressive self-representation in Sophia's letters which become a haunting for her and her family. The first is her explanation of her metamorphosis in Orientalist terms, and the second is her description of a hiatus in writing her letters as an

---

25. Valenti, *Sophia Peabody Vol. 1,* 86.
26. Valenti, *Sophia Peabody Vol. 1,* 85.
27. For a discussion of how Sophia struggled with being believed at home, see García, "'With the Eyes That Are Given Me,'" 73.

apparent "exorcism," building on the trope of being possessed by forces beyond her control. Valenti points to how the interruption in the letters between January 20 and March 11, 1835 came "at the very height of her social whirlwind, at the very moment of Mrs. Peabody's gravest concern," and how the silence "triggered enormous concerns [in her mother] about sexual impropriety" on Sophia's part.[28] Valenti recounts how Mrs. Peabody's alarm was increased to its highest pitch because of Sophia's exultant and too-close friendship with a Cuban planter's son, Fernando Zayas, which raised in the mother fears of seduction and "unholy" dalliances.[29]

Such concerns were continually fanned by Sophia, who, in keeping with her self-representation as a kind of biblical Eve born into a Cuban Eden, often referred to the world she saw as being "made new" each morning. She linked this feeling of newness to the speedy improvements in her health that she underwent while on the island. Only a month into her life in Cuba, in a February 3, 1834 letter, Sophia comments on her project of well-being and its early success:

> Regular exercise in the fresh dawn of day & at sunset, with a temperature so equal, soft & pure, must eventually have a genial effect—I must not omit telling you that my *nights* are better than they ever were—I am not so disturbed with terrific visions & seldom wake after I am once asleep, which is pretty soon after I go to bed [. . .] Moreover, I am *drowsy* very often, which is an entirely new condition of being to me, & proves beyond doubt that Nature is beginning to rest herself after such a desperate action & wakefulness of years. [. . .] I always felt in a perfectly unnatural state of existence in the north. I can compare it to nothing but being suspended between heaven and earth like Mahomet's tomb. (25, emphasis in original)

This passage is worth quoting at length because of how Sophia creates a binary opposition between the US North and Cuba, noting how her previous life at home was plagued by insomnia, desperation, and agony. What was "unnatural" in the North becomes natural in the tropics, separating her sensibilities from those of her native country and assimilating her into Cuba's geoculture.

---

28. Valenti, *Sophia Peabody Vol. 1,* 64.
29. Valenti, *Sophia Peabody Vol. 1,* 65.

Her choice of Orientalist language—in comparing her liminal state between two worlds to "Mahomet's tomb"—further reflects an element of the discourses of transamericanity. This literary choice is relevant because she deploys it within Cuba, which was both a colony of Spain and assiduously desired by the United States. This is one passage in which we see how Sophia's brand of US literary Orientalism develops in Cuba, where she says she awakes each morning "in a blaze of glory & strength" (25). This awakening to boundless energy and revitalizing (rather than destructive) emotion is a thread she weaves through the *Cuba Journal,* providing a sense of how she saw the island as the geo-cultural catalyst of her transformation.

Her rapid metamorphosis from a near invalid into an adventurous woman eager for all kinds of stimulation soon caused her family to become doubtful of the truthfulness of her stories. As she notes in a May 11, 1834 letter, "It is indeed true that I am the maiden of prowess I boast to be—that is—that I do indeed ride on horseback & in volante—that I *do* walk off to draw trees—& that I *can* tell of sound sleep such as I have not realized since childhood" (83, emphasis in original). The exultation that was so difficult for her family to understand resulted from Sophia's representation of her body as a source of physical and emotional pleasure rather than an enemy, as she had represented it for most of her earlier life. The emphasis in the phrases "I do" and "I can" not only denote agency and strong will, they also underscore her desire to persuade her family of the change that began almost immediately after she set foot in Cuba. That Sophia frequently rode on horseback or traveled in small carriages built for speed (the famous Cuban *volantes*), or that she took miles-long walks "to draw trees," must have seemed nearly fantastical to family and friends who had known her for most of her life as sickly and bed-ridden.

In addition to the transgressive overtones of her literary descriptions, Sophia appropriates Mary's notion that she is possessed and adds fuel to that fire. Also in that letter, Sophia goes on to say: "If ever I was possessed—it was that morning, with an ecstatic demon—I could not be contained in my little chamber" (592). That opposition between being "contained" and being "ecstatic," which Mary saw as demonic, is at the center of Sophia's metamorphosis in Cuba. Writing was a product of her "effervescing emotions" (592), a combination of her unfettered need to express herself and her desire for attention, both of which were frowned upon by her family. At that moment in Cuba, she is elated that, upon "frisking" out into the hall, disappointed at seeing only a dog, she eventually finds one of the many visitors to the plantation drinking coffee. Sophia writes: "My apparition was so unexpected & sudden—& in white too—that I verily believe he thought I was a spirit" (592). Her choice to dismiss Mary's expressed concern about her "demonic" possession, and turn it instead into a playful description of her continued and growing elation in Cuba, invests this volume of the journal with some of its strongest gothicized tensions. Even by the end of her time in Cuba, Sophia did not shy away from flaunting the state of emotional excess that her relatives—mother and sister especially—deplored and cautioned her against.

The final gothicization in Sophia's letters I focus on here is her description of an interruption in her writing. Building on the trope of possession, Sophia blames the two-month gap in the journal, when she did not write at all, on an "exorcism" by Mary. In a March 11, 1835 letter, she writes:

> Since the 20th of January you have received no news from me—Mary, by talking to me about the time journalizing absorbed, exorcised completely all my spirit about it, so that after I wrote through my Reserva experiences, I came to a dead halt. (610)

It was after her visit to another plantation, Reserva, to which Sophia traveled alone without Mary, that her writing reached a climax of exultation about the lifestyle she enjoyed in Cuba. After that visit and the journal descriptions that ensued, Mary appears to have put her foot down in an attempt to silence Sophia's journal. However, Sophia breaks her promise to Mary, admitting that she resumed her "journalizing" and that she kept "a slight memorandum of every day since," which suggests that she did not completely stop herself from writing, as her sister would have had her do. Sophia appears to have made daily notes to herself, biding her time until she knew she could take up her pen once more.

The repeated gothicized representation of the act of writing as evil in Sophia's case shows how her passion for writing was perceived as an obsession, something she had to break with for her own good. That Sophia chose to pretend she stopped writing rather than actually give up her journalizing shows how her letters had become an important creative venue for her literary self-expression. This need may have resulted from the fact that the letters were her way of challenging cultural expectations while having the distance of an ocean between her actions and how they were perceived and judged back home. Daniela Ciani Forza has noted how for Sophia "being in Cuba meant facing the challenge of her own New England background and her own personal search for self-realization."[30] But Sophia did much more than fuse "her New England education with equally strong inspirations drawn from Cuban landscapes and life," as Forza suggests.[31] Sophia not just challenged but even transgressed her New England upbringing, choosing to privilege her newfound agency in Cuba. That exultant transgression is what makes her text especially unique among the many nineteenth-century writings about the island.

Indeed, the transgressive haunting of Sophia's *Cuba Journal* life is such that, while scholars have traced the influence her letters had on her husband's work—in Hawthorne's "Rappaccini's Daughter," as one example—she basically erased Cuba from how she wished to be remembered.[32] As I have discussed, her constant physical activity, her ecstatic appreciation of Cuban flora, sunsets, and moonlit nights, and her enthusiastic socializing among the island's slave-owning plantocracy, metamorphosized Sophia from a near invalid into a "maiden of prowess," as she described herself (83). Indeed, in her last letter home from Cuba, Sophia categorized the effect that her visit to the island would have on her life as transformative. In the March 31, 1835 letter, Sophia again described her usual rides on horseback and her love for the landscape, writing:

> Oh what an inheritance will be the memory of these dawn rides to my heart in coming times—How beautifully Nature educates the soul—If I do not find myself *better—really* better—if in ever so small

---

30. Forza, "Sophia Peabody Hawthorne's 'Cuba Journal,'" 88.
31. Forza, "Sophia Peabody Hawthorne's 'Cuba Journal,'" 88.
32. Valenti notes that the "gardens, the woman so luxuriantly portrayed and intimately associated with flowers, the father doctor whose meddling with plans exceeds the boundaries of propriety" are all "prefigured" in the *Cuba Journal*. In addition, Valenti has also discussed the influence of Sophia's representations of the tropics in "Rappaccini's Daughter." Valenti, *Sophia Peabody Vol. 1*, 218, 222.

a degree—after this year in Cuba—I shall think that I am harder than flint— (624, emphasis in original)

As I have already argued elsewhere, Sophia's early transcendentalism moved beyond connecting Nature to a mediation between herself and the divine, engaging in consistently transgressive assertions of female power.[33] However, and unlike her hopes in this letter, once she returned to her parents' home in New England, Sophia's fears of being resistant to change came true, as most of the improvement to her health from the Cuba visit vanished. Valenti points out that "Sophia had blossomed in Cuba" but upon her return to Salem, she "repress[ed] and repudiate[ed] the person she had become," resulting in her regression "into a pain-ridden, struggling artist."[34] This physical reversion and her emotional aversion to her self-representation in Cuba suggest the transgressive hues that help explain why the *Cuba Journal* haunted Sophia.

In like manner, and because it is based on the sisters's letters from Cuba, Mary's *Juanita* also has been categorized as having gothic elements. Patricia Ard, in the introduction to her edition of the novel in 2000, states that the work "evokes the Gothic" by replacing the lonely castle with "the equally isolated plantation house," and by constantly disrupting peaceful domestic moments with abrupt and violent scenes of slave torture.[35] Ard further points to the claustrophobic confinement and isolation experienced by the novel's heroine, Helen Wentworth, and identifies other gothic undertones in the repeated instances within the novel when the family, as a symbol of moral education, is "perversely corrupted [. . .] in the service of slavery."[36] John Havard also has noted how Mary's novel is "a sentimental, oftentimes Gothic excoriation of 1830s Cuban slavery," and how some characters are used to represent a "Gothic Cuba."[37] This representation of the island as a gothicized geography corrupted by slavery is part of how, by building on Sophia's self-representations, Mary contributed to crafting Cuba as a gothic geoculture.

---

33. García, "'With the Eyes that Are Given Me,'" 60.
34. Valenti, *Sophia Peabody Vol. 1*, 107.
35. Ard, "Introduction," xxvii.
36. Ard, "Introduction," xxviii.
37. Havard, "Mary Peabody Mann's 'Juanita,'" 144, 147.

A long-time educator, who later married US education pioneer Horace Mann, Mary used gothic tropes to warn her readers about the geoculture of slavery, seeking to sow fear about the national corruption that would inevitably result from acquiring Cuba as a colonial possession. Published several decades after the US Civil War and a year after the abolition of slavery in Cuba, Mary's text conjures the ghost of Cuban slavery to warn against how Cuba, even after slavery was abolished, was still pernicious. In his analysis, Havard argues that the novel is interested in "the intersections between [US] slavery and expansionism," and identifies the text as a historical romance that explores "how the past constitutes the present."[38] Indeed, Mary gravitated to the gothic because, as a genre, it functioned easily as an intersection between factuality and fiction, especially in connection to slavery. Anticipating the emergence of a US empire in the Americas by more than a decade, as Havard suggests, the novel sought to revive anxieties over renewed colonial desire for Cuba. For Mary, the Cubans were "a people so nationally ignorant," so inherently tainted by slavery and colonialism, that they were incapable of remaking themselves in the image of the United States. Against this backdrop, her novel uses slavery as a transgressive haunting so that it becomes a warning to forestall the future evil of its potential influence on the United States.

By the 1880s, the gothicized penumbra we glean in Sophia's *Cuba Journal* morphs into a full gothic shading in Mary's novel. One main way in which *Juanita* diverges from Sophia's "Cuba Journal," its nonfictional master text, is by establishing Cuba and the United States as binary opposites so that Cuba functions as a negative double.[39] Though Mary used Sophia's journal as primary source material, she altered the opposition between Cuba and the United States to represent the island as a noxious influence on white US women and on white or mixed-race Cuban women. In Mary's novel, this negative doubling is evident in the opposition between Helen, the protagonist modeled after Mary herself, and three Cuban women characters: Isabella, Helen's friend and

---

38. Havard, "Mary Peabody Mann's 'Juanita,'" 145.

39. Havard, in his essay comparing Peabody Mann's novel with Martin R. Delany's *Blake*, which I discussed in chapter 2, argues that "[US] superiority is particularly exemplified, for Mann, in New England, depicted as the representatively national space and as a retreat from Gothic Cuban terror." Havard, "Mary Peabody Mann's *Juanita* and Martin R. Delany's *Blake*," 513.

a slave owner's wife; Juanita, the mixed-race character for whom the novel is named; and Camilla, the "dark" slave, who embodies the monstrousness of Cuba's geoculture and its dangerousness to the future of the United States. All three of these women represent main transgressors of gendered cultural norms (represented by Helen as the ideal), whether knowingly or not. While both Isabella and Juanita perish by the end of the novel, for different but related reasons (both connected to slavery), Camilla endures, underscoring a message about the troubling resilience of the island's worst influence.

Helen, a Protestant New England orphan educated at a US school for girls, travels to Cuba to visit Isabella, her former classmate, who is married to the slave-owning Marquis de Rodriguez. From the novel's start, the relationship between Helen and Isabella allegorizes the connection between the United States and Cuba, especially since Isabella was educated in New England and maintained her friendship with Helen even after returning to her native island.[40] Havard observes that "Helen metonymically represents [US] values, values [Mary] sees as being particularly present in New England but which more generally characterize the [US] national narrative the novel invokes."[41] True to Mary's purpose in the narrative, Helen soon realizes that Isabella has been corrupted by the sensuous comforts the geoculture of slavery enables. Helen's portrayal as a New England teacher, and Isabella's as a corrupted Cuban version of the Spanish aristocracy, exemplify this opposition between a progressive United States and a defunct Old World class system, which Mary saw replicated in Cuban society. As Havard has argued, Mary takes personal experience and turns it into a national argument about culture and identity. In turn, these representations call to mind the divergent reactions that Mary and Sophia had to their experiences in Cuba, where the latter was perceived as having been negatively influenced by her life on the island.

In establishing the key contrast in the novel between Helen and Isabella, Mary foregrounds Helen's antislavery activism (much like her

---

40. By representing Isabella as a US-educated Cuban of the planter class, Peabody Mann evidences some knowledge of Cuban society. By the 1840s, educated Cubans "had been sending their sons to US schools or universities for a generation," and many in the planter class were annexationists, who wanted Cuba to become part of the United States. Thomas, *Cuba*, 209.

41. Havard, "Mary Peabody Mann's 'Juanita,'" 153.

own) and repeatedly juxtaposes it with what she represents as Isabella's moral paralysis (similar to what she perceived as Sophia's own attitudes toward slavery). This opposition is highlighted when Helen and Isabella go horseback riding and stumble across "a scene characteristic of slave institutions, even under the mildest regulation." The gory image that "bursts upon" Helen is described in graphic detail by the narrator:

> A group of colored men and women were standing under a tree, to which was chained an infuriated blood-hound, from whose sides blood streamed upon the ground. Two negroes, also attached to a post, at a little distance from the dog, by long ropes, stood bleeding and apparently exhausted; one held a whip, which was stained with the animal's blood. (73)

The scene is given with little context or explanation so that readers find themselves in the same position as Helen, unfamiliar and shocked observers who must figure out what is occurring before they can understand its significance.

Soon Helen realizes that the slaves are being forced to torture the dogs so that the animals learn to focus their attacks only on black slaves.[42] The purpose of this training in the use of the infamous Cuban bloodhounds is so that the overseer can boast "that the white man is never bitten in my plantation" (73). Upon this gruesome realization, Helen faints, falling "heavily upon Isabella's arm, and slid[ing] to the ground in happy unconsciousness" (74). Although Helen comes close to fainting several times in the novel, this is the one moment when she actually loses consciousness. While fainting is a common trope in sentimental and gothic fiction, usually signaling the heroine's evasion of a threat to her sexual purity, in Helen's case the threat is to her status as a white US woman, whose moral convictions lead her to reject any participation, even as an unwitting observer, in such a scene. The fact that she faints while Isabella remains conscious further contrasts Helen's sensibilities with the hardened attitude of the Cuban woman.

Isabella's function as Helen's negative double becomes more apparent as Helen fails in her attempts to persuade her friend that she must

---

42. Peabody Mann here demonstrates some familiarity with Cuban society. For a description of how the "Cuban bloodhound" was trained through this method to hunt slaves, see Ballou, *History of Cuba*.

remain true to her US education and renounce the impact of slavery on her life. In this way, the novel suggests, the geoculture of slavery irrevocably infects even those who have been positively influenced by the United States. The narrator explains: "When Isabella first returned to Cuba, she was plunged into scenes and modes of life which she had wholly forgotten [. . .] If it had not been for her constant intercourse with Helen, her American life might have become to her as a dream" (50). This moment is one of the first that connects Isabella to Sophia's experience in Cuba. As Helen sees happening with Isabella, we know from Sophia's letters and from biographical accounts how Mary constantly had to remind Sophia of her "American life," and of the duties she owed to herself and her family.

The intertextual relationship between Mary's novel and the *Cuba Journal* is clearly evident when the narrator describes Isabella "as an artist," who enjoys sketching nature, very much like Sophia did. When Helen begins to ask questions about slave torture, given that she believes the slaves to be "a kindly race," Isabella's response is: "But let us not talk of them any more now. I am afraid you will not observe all the beauties around you. Is not my rose hedge beautiful?" This reluctance to discuss slavery and to focus, instead, on the aesthetics of the surrounding landscape, echoes Sophia's attitude in Cuba. As Sophia's letters demonstrate, she often remarked on the beauty of the Morrells' extensive gardens, praising their ornate structure without acknowledging the fact that the coerced labor of enslaved men and women made them so perfect.

Unlike Sophia, however, who constantly complained about Mary's criticisms but showed little desire to alter her behavior, Isabella changes because of Helen's insistence that she give up her passive behavior toward slavery. The narrator says that through Helen's influence Isabella "for the first time" recognized how she had become "apathetic [. . .] under an accepted wrong" (32). The novel credits Helen, "and circumstances of unusual occurrence," for "breaking the spell" and reviving in Isabella "all her youthful abhorrence of slavery [so that she] could never 'make the best of it' again, after looking upon it through Helen's eyes" (68, 106). However, this seeing through Helen's eyes ultimately costs Isabella her life since she quickly begins to waste away of an unspecified illness. Although Mary knew that Sophia was not about to lose her earthly life because of her attitude toward slavery in Cuba,

Isabella's similarities to Sophia function as a warning about the moral cost of what Mary saw as Sophia's acquiescence to the geoculture of slavery.

In addition to killing off Isabella, Mary's novel further warns against the threat to white US authority created by contact with the geoculture of slavery in Cuba through the slave character of Camilla. Represented as looking like an "orang-outang"—a description taken verbatim from Sophia's own portrayal of a slave in the *Cuba Journal*—Camilla is also devious, willful, and deceitful.[43] She routinely floods the floors of the plantation house with the excuse of thoroughly cleaning them, as a way to exasperate Isabella, and to prevent the family from having free access to their favorite rooms for extended periods of time. At one point, Isabella tells Camilla's story to Helen, noting how the slave "was spoiled" before she arrived at their plantation by a former overseer who "ruined her" by giving her authority. Isabella states that Camilla and the overseer "became such tyrants together that the whole rule was taken from the master's hands, till on one occasion they ventured a little too far, and [the overseer] was dismissed, and Camilla was sent into the field" so that her proud spirit could be broken (67). The novel thus calls attention to Camilla—represented as an intelligent and empowered slave—as the text's Gothic monstrosity, an aberration that should not be allowed to exist.

To achieve this, the novel refocuses the clash between Helen and Isabella onto the conflict between the latter and Camilla, subverting the master-slave power dynamics. Isabella concludes her story about Camilla by stating: "Since my régime she has taken me for her slave; but she is so useful I cannot do without her and when my children are ill she is like one inspired. She is never so well content as when the power is all in her own hands" (67). Describing herself as enslaved by Camilla, Isabella for the first time persuades Helen to sympathize with her. Helen agrees that Isabella is "under bondage, indeed," and asks her friend's forgiveness for having repeatedly reproached her for her passivity toward slavery. Helen generally has little patience with Isabella, but she is empathetic when the latter casts herself in the role of the slave and Camilla in the role of enslaver. This suggests that the geoculture of slavery warps the master-slave relationship so that the asymme-

---

43. In an October 1, 1834 letter, Sophia describes Tecla, the Morrells' slave, as having "ourang-outang arms" (344).

try of power becomes thwarted by the enslavers' need for the enslaved, who in turn is empowered to enslave the enslaver.

Helen may be an abolitionist in the United States, but because Camilla is cast as the villain, in Cuba the tables are turned and it is Isabella whom Helen pities. This moment suggests a weakness in Helen because she accepts the distorted image of Isabella's role as reflected in Cuba's geocultural mirror. Helen, by feeling sympathy for Isabella instead of Camilla, is drawn into the ideology of slavery. Further, Isabella here functions not only as a character who has been corrupted by the geoculture of slavery, but also as someone who can, in turn, spread that corruption to the novel's US heroine. However, the narrative is careful to imply that, despite any possible sympathy elicited in Helen, it is Isabella's incompetence in commanding her domestic sphere that bestows power onto Camilla. Thus, the story suggests that Isabella is transgressing her assigned domain of influence and authority in the household by relinquishing her duties as a white US-educated Cuban woman, while Camilla is a concomitant transgressor for appropriating an authority that would not be assigned to her as a slave. When Helen asks Isabella why she does not get rid of Camilla, the latter replies: "Because she knows how to do everything, and I cannot keep house without her" (79). The geoculture of slavery provides Isabella with a life of luxury, but the novel proposes that the price for that privilege is a slave-like dependence that functions as a dangerous reverse bondage.

Isabella's character shows how slavery promotes a psychological enslavement—in keeping with how transamericanity works in this geocultural context—that destabilizes the very racial hierarchy on which the institution depends. Because she is a slave, Camilla would have little actual power, but Mary wants her readers to identify with Isabella and to fear their own, and their nation's, corruption under the influence of slavery and its legacy. After listening to this, Helen once more exclaims: "What a life of slavery it is for you!" (79). Indeed, Isabella's inability to meet her responsibility as the moral compass of the household by bequeathing power over her home on the rebellious Camilla, points us to the apparent reason for Isabella's inexplicable illness and death in the novel.[44] Ard notes that Isabella's "ambiguous wasting ill-

---

44. Cooper argues that the fact that "Mann kills off Isabella serves as a testimony to the inadequacy of the role that she represents." See Cooper, "'Should Not These Things Be Known?'" 154.

ness," which she contracts after she begins disagreeing with Helen, results from Isabella's "inability to square her life with the horrors of slavery."[45]

In keeping with the novel's gothicized tones, however, the reasons behind Isabella's death seem more complex. Helen says that although she can see no remedy for Isabella's pain, she perceives a "moral darkness" closing in around her friend. This darkening that Helen perceives is a metaphorical allusion to Isabella's racialization or "blackening" by the geoculture of slavery (a trope Louisa May Alcott also drew upon in her own representations of Cuba's influence, as I discussed in the previous chapter), and also to her abdication of her US-based moral power. By ceding control to a black slave of her domestic sphere—originally run according to the US principles she learned from her New England education—Isabella "darkens" herself, transgressing her role as the moral educator of her household. The novel suggests that US principles are not invulnerable and must be protected against Cuba's corruptive influence, represented through the interrelatedness of Camilla and Isabella's transgressions.

This conflict between Isabella and Camilla is recast a final time in the representation of Juanita, the title character. When Isabella initially introduces Helen to Juanita, she describes the latter as a "Moor" and an *emancipada,* or legally freed slave. While actually free, Juanita remains in slave-like servitude because of her secret love for Ludovico, the eldest son of Isabella and the Marquis, who is heir to the slave plantation. Juanita's characterization as a freed former slave willing to remain enslaved because of her love for the slave master's son points to another way in which the novel links the geoculture of slavery to psychological enslavement. While Juanita is no longer a slave by law, she willingly gives up her liberty, evidencing a similar type of subjugation to that which Isabella articulates, and which leads the title character to remain as the Rodríguez's slave rather than being free.

In addition to occupying a liminal space between slavery and freedom, Juanita is repeatedly racialized in the text as "not black." But because she is of African descent, Juanita knows that her love for Ludovico cannot be because she exists in an in-between where she is not quite white and "not black." In this way, Mary casts Juanita as a

---

45. Ard, "Introduction," xxvii.

"tragic mulatta" figure crafted to articulate anxieties about racial mixing as a consequence of slavery.[46] Further, because Juanita is Cuban, I also read her as allegorizing the island's own in-between state (caught between Spanish colonialism and US imperial desire). Thus, Juanita (like her native island) cannot benefit from Helen's intervention because she is doomed both by her racialized gender and by her colonial status. In the novel, Juanita's fatal connection to the geoculture of slavery vests her with a doubly tragic fate. Juanita cannot join the white social establishment (either in Cuba or in the United States), which will never accept her because of her mixed race, and she is also marked by her status as a colonial subject of Spain on an island desired by the United States as a colonial possession.

The novel suggests that Juanita's mental bondage is more dangerous than physical enslavement, and, therefore, Juanita becomes a cautionary tale for women (slave and free) who are influenced by Cuba. Juanita's psychological colonization becomes more evident after Ludovico finds himself a widower upon the death of Carolina, his US-educated, white Cuban wife. Early in the novel, Ludovico falls in love with Carolina, who after her return to Cuba from the United States (and just like Isabella's negative transformation on the island) begins to exhibit an overtly sensual and frivolous demeanor, as well as particularly cruel behavior toward the slaves. As in Isabella's case, this change is connected to Cuba's gothic geoculture, which exerts a deadly influence on women. In his study of the novel, Havard notes how "the depraved Carolina epitomizes Gothic Cuba, and her entrance into the Rodriguez family contributes to its ruin."[47] Carolina dies in childbirth, followed shortly thereafter by Isabella, and after the latter's death, Helen takes Ludovico, Juanita, and Isabella's younger children to the United States, where Ludovico suddenly realizes that he loves Juanita, and proposes marriage. Juanita refuses but pledges her eternal servitude to Ludovico and agrees to return with him to Cuba. Following the "tragic mulatta" trope, Juanita claims she would "be a dark cloud upon his life," a claim with which Helen does not disagree. In this way, Juanita's character allegorizes Cuba's own gothicized fate within the novel's uni-

---

46. For a discussion of the "tragic mulatta" trope, see Berzon, *Neither White Nor Black* and Raimon, *The "Tragic Mulatta" Revisited*.

47. Havard, "Mary Peabody Mann's 'Juanita,'" 147.

verse, as she cannot be redeemed because she is ultimately doomed by the imbricated relationship between her race, gender, and nationality.

Juanita, the most subservient of the non-white characters in the novel, plays a heightened tragic role because she is actually neither a slave nor a rebel, like Camilla. When Ludovico and Juanita return to Cuba, she is kidnapped by slave catchers, and taken to a location where new and former slaves have been imprisoned. There, Juanita is killed off-scene in a fire set by an angry mob that suspects the slaves of conspiring to revolt. In this way, the novel suggests that Juanita must die because she has transgressed against cultural norms by believing she is more than what the geoculture of slavery reduces her to—a slave whose life is always at the mercy of her enslavers. After Juanita's death, the narrator describes Ludovico's desire to become a "good" slave master in Cuba, and ends with an appeal to the reader to have faith "that God teaches man by his failures as well as by success and happiness" (211, 216, 222). It is through Juanita's "ghost," or the memory of her tragic fate, that Mary attempts to persuade readers that Helen's inability to alter the lives of any transgressive Cuban woman should serve as a caution that the United States should leave the island alone.

What is most intriguing about Mary's stereotyped representation of Juanita is that she, like Isabella, is given traits of character that can be easily traced back to Sophia in her letters. Like Sophia in real life, Juanita demonstrates what Isabella describes as "a wonderful genius for painting." Isabella explains that she uses the word genius on purpose to describe Juanita because "the word talent does not describe [Juanita's ability]." In Juanita's portfolios, Isabella notes, "you will find the night-blooming cereus, our gigantic ceyba tree, and, indeed, all the peculiar tropical plants" (78). Mary does this by referring not only to Juanita's "genius"—a word often used by Sophia's family to describe her own artistic talent—but also to specific drawings of the night-blooming cereus and the ceiba, which Sophia mentioned in her letters.[48] The question that arises for me in relation to this passage is why Mary

---

48. In a February 14, 1834 letter, Sophia remarks on "One ceyba we passed which exceeded any thing I ever conceived of in the way of a production of the earth. It seemed to have more to do with heaven, and I looked up at its giant height and semi-circle of eternal green with an emotion of reverence and awe, that I seldom feel toward any thing inanimate" (34–35). See also Badaracco, "'The Night-Blooming Cereus': A Letter from the 'Cuba Journal.'"

would so evidently represent Juanita with the exact same talents everyone in their circle of family and friends knew Sophia had, especially if they had read the *Cuba Journal*, where these words appear almost verbatim. Ard suggests that the fact that the Morrell family was still living may have been the driving force behind Mary's refusal to publish *Juanita* until after her death, but perhaps it was the transgressive change she witnessed in Sophia, which she represented in her novel, that contributed to Mary's reticence. By associating her sister's characteristics in the *Cuba Journal* with two main characters who are killed in the novel—Isabella in her unwillingness to face the horrors of slavery and Juanita in her artistic genius—Mary represented Cuba as the site that had effectively extinguished Sophia's New England character. For Mary, Cuba had led Sophia both to abandon her painting and to be complicit with the geoculture of slavery.

Mary's concern over the potential corruption Cuba could inflict on the United States was fueled by the metamorphosis she witnessed and tried to discourage in Sophia. Once the sisters returned to New England, this difference over the question of slavery set them wider apart, with Mary becoming a vocal abolitionist while Sophia took on a more conservative and non-interventionist position, similar to that of Hawthorne, her famous husband. Perhaps it was this easily drawn association (for those familiar with the *Cuba Journal*) between her characters and Sophia that Mary also feared in publication, even after her younger sister's death in 1871. In the same way that Sophia herself suppressed the *Cuba Journal*, refusing to have it published, Mary may have been similarly haunted and therefore prevented her novel from going to press before her own death in 1887.[49] This haunting is especially poignant because, by the novel's end, both Isabella and Juanita are dead, punished for their different, if ultimately similar, transgressions produced by the geoculture of slavery. It may be that in giving Juanita and Isabella Sophia's most salient characteristics—especially her artistic sensibilities and her mostly passive attitude toward slavery—Mary also wanted to express her own fear that Sophia's alteration while in Cuba reflected a process of assimilation as dangerous to the

---

49. Valenti has found that when Sophia looked into whether it "'would do to print'" the *Cuba Journal*, she "rejected the idea," noting, "There is so much about people in them." Valenti, *Sophia Peabody Vol. 2*, 265.

US national identity as the mixing of races was perceived to be before, during, and after the US Civil War.

While Havard suggests that Mary was ambivalent toward the US acquisition of Cuba, and although the narrator addresses the notion that the United States could save Cuba from its self-destructive ways, I see the novel as taking a clearly anti-annexationist position. Once Isabella is dead and Helen takes the children and Juanita to New England, the narrator uneasily argues that US annexation of Cuba is the only "hope of change" for that island:

> Another difficulty [in Cuba] is that of making innovations among a people so nationally ignorant as the inhabitants of the Spanish Colonies. No hope of such a change existed, except in the possibility of annexation to the United States [. . .] The United States desired the annexation [of Cuba] for commercial and political interests, but these advantages would be accompanied by many evils [. . .]. (201)

Within the novel's ideology, the fact that Cuba is a Spanish colony dooms the island (like Juanita herself) because its people's ignorance is perceived as racially inherent, and therefore insurmountable.

The novel articulates a racial prejudice that transmutes into a national one because it is not only the non-white nature of Juanita that is problematic, but also the fact that she is influenced by Spanish culture. The novel's critique of Cuba as a specifically Spanish colony is closely related to the fear of racial mixing within the geoculture of slavery, to the legacies of the "Black Legend," and to its derivative nature as a copy of Old World structures of power and sentiment. Mary's narrative posits that the geoculture of slavery makes Spanish colonials inferior, especially those who are darker in the spectrum of nineteenth-century racial politics. In addressing US slavery, both before and after Emancipation, the narrator recognizes how former US slaves obtained education and rose above their initial bondage. But Mary does not grant the same ability to Cuban slaves (despite, or perhaps because of, Camilla's representation as insubordinate). The narrator points out that US Americans who supported annexation as a way to save Cuba from its "sad state of anarchy" did not know that others among them wanted annexation to "extend the area of slavery" prior to abolition (214). In that way, Mary argues for a transamerican connection between the slave-based geocultures of the US South and Cuba. Here, the gothicized representations of slavery connect the United States and the Spanish Caribbean, becoming a strong argument against US colonialism in Cuba.

Using gothic tropes, Mary fictionalized the horrors of slavery that she witnessed firsthand in Cuba. Ard has suggested that *Juanita* lacks a place in the canon of antislavery texts because of its publication long after abolition.[50] More recently, Maria Windell has pointed to how the novel's "political visions were not made obsolete by its abolitionist campaign [for] while its prominent antislavery narrative may have been outdated by 1887, the novel still engages both abolition and annexation in terms that anticipate 1898."[51] Along similar lines, Havard finds that *Juanita*'s significance lies not in its seemingly belated antislavery stance, but more in its representation of US colonial ambitions for Cuba.[52] I argue, however, that *Juanita*'s significance also resides in its gothicized representation of Cuba, based on Sophia's and Mary's actual experiences. That mix between actuality and fiction points us to the ways in which the gothic served to narrativize the "real" in intelligible and persuasive ways, especially in relation to "foreign" locations, like Cuba. Further, because in the case of both the *Cuba Journal* and *Juanita* their authors did not want their works published during their lifetimes, the Cuba that they both similarly shared and differently constructed becomes a transgressive haunting for the entire time period between Sophia's first letters and Mary's posthumous publication of her novel.

In direct relation to a rising US empire in the nineteenth century, Ann Laura Stoller has noted how "to be haunted" means "to be frequented by and possessed by a force that not always bares a proper name."[53] Because of its transgressive representations, Sophia's *Cuba Journal* haunted both its author and her sister, especially since these transgressions become major preoccupations in Mary's novelized rewriting of the journal. The transgressive hauntings produced by

---

50. Ard, "Introduction," xi.
51. Windell, "Moor, *Mulata*, Mulatta," 307.
52. Havard, "Mary Peabody Mann's 'Juanita,'" 145.
53. Stoller, *Haunted by Empire*, 1.

Cuba's gothic geoculture in the Peabody sisters were filled with threatening echoes and resonances that spanned the hemisphere, the century, and their lives. By attending to the fraught relationship between these narratives, and to how and why they gothicized Cuba, we answer Stoller's call to assign proper names to the forces within transamericanity that haunted the hemisphere during the nineteenth century.

CHAPTER FOUR

Gothic Emplotments

Cirilo Villaverde's *Cecilia Valdés* and
The Story of Evangelina Cisneros, Told by Herself

IN HIS famous novel *Cecilia Valdés; or, El Angel Hill*, Cirilo Villaverde initially describes his titular heroine in gothicized ways.[1] An anticolonial rebel who supported filibustering efforts to free Cuba from Spain, Villaverde was jailed for his complicity but escaped from prison to the United States, where he spent more than thirty years in exile, and where he rewrote his novel.[2] In describing his protagonist as a young

---

1. I refer to Villaverde's 1882 revision of his 1839 version of *Cecilia Valdés*, which was originally published as a two-part series in a Cuban periodical. The lengthier revised version was published forty-three years later in New York. Lazo, *Writing to Cuba*, 171. In arguing for an understanding of Villaverde's novel as "part of the origin of nineteenth-century Cuban literature," Luis has highlighted how the 1882 text is nearly a complete rewriting of the two previous, shorter versions published in 1839. Luis, "*Cecilia Valdés*," 15. In this chapter, I use the 2005 Oxford University Press translation but provide longer block quotes in both the original Spanish and English translation.

2. Villaverde met Narciso López (who led two filibustering expeditions to Cuba in 1850 and 1851) in 1848 and actively conspired with the latter to overthrow Spanish rule on the island. The conspiracy was betrayed to the Spaniards by the US government, and Villaverde was arrested and convicted of conspiring against Spain. "In a daring escape worthy of one of his novels, Villaverde walked out of jail [. . .], boarded a ship for Florida, and made his way to New York." He remained in the United States until his death in 1894. Lazo, *Writing to Cuba*, 172.

93

girl, Villaverde notes how Cecilia's "face belonged to the same type as that of the virgins of the most renowned painters," but then adds that her "small mouth and full lips [indicated] voluptuousness rather than strength of character" (12–13). This racialized depiction suggests Cecilia possesses more sexual power than moral fortitude, and is followed by the narrator noticing that her "plump round cheeks and a dimple in the middle of her chin formed an attractive whole, which in order to be perfect lacked only a less spiteful if not downright wicked expression" (13). In this way, Villaverde crafts Cecilia's character as embodying a disparity between what she appears to be and what she actually is, investing his novel's heroine with a gothicized duality from the start.

Fifteen years later, *The Story of Evangelina Cisneros, Told by Herself* was penned by Evangelina Betancourt Cossío y Cisneros, who was "rescued" from a Cuban prison by a *New York Journal* reporter and brought to the United States.[3] Cisneros, daughter of an anticolonial rebel, was imprisoned for her own subversive actions against Spain and became a cause célèbre when the *New York Journal* orchestrated her escape. In her "alleged autobiography," as Teresa Prados-Torreira has described the narrative produced and promoted by the *Journal,* Cisneros is figured within the text as the gendered embodiment of a Cuba imperiled by Spain.[4] Unlike Cecilia, whom Villaverde racializes as having African blood, Cisneros is whitened but still gothicized as a damsel in distress who would have perished without the heroic intervention of her US rescuers. However, when she tells her own story—included after an introduction by Julian Hawthorne (Sophia Peabody Hawthorne's son) and after her rescuer's account—Cisneros both exploits and challenges this gothicized figuration.

In this chapter, I examine Villaverde's characterization of his heroine in *Cecilia Valdés*—widely recognized as the most important nineteenth-century Cuban novel—and Cisneros's representation in Hawthorne's introduction and in her own account, to show the shift in gothic tropes about Cuba within this time period. This discursive transition went from Villaverde's heroine's representation as corrupted because she is of mixed race—similar to other writers in this study—to

---

3. Leary notes that Cisneros "was broken out of prison by agents of the *Journal,* perhaps by simple bribery; the paper publicized its own account of its reporter's daring rescue raid." Leary, *A Cultural History,* 100.

4. Prados-Torreira, *Mambisas,* 143.

Cisneros's whitening as a gothicized victim of Spain in need of rescue by the United States.[5] Although the rhetorical goals of these figurations differed, they similarly promoted—and challenged—what I describe as a *gothic emplotment,* which signified Cuba through similar narrative structures that fused race, gender, and nationality to represent Cuban women as dangerous or as in danger. This emplotment functioned within the geoculture of slavery as part of the discursive structures of transamericanity produced and disseminated by century's end.

Both Villaverde and Cisneros's stories, the first a fictionalized novel purportedly based on fact, and the other a supposedly factual autobiography, share three main elements within their paradigms of emplotment:

- First, and like other narratives in this study, these accounts rely on a claim of factuality, which connects them to how slavery and the gothic became linked to each other in this hemisphere.
- Both narratives also promote a representational commonplace that imbricates race, gender, and nationality as ontologically problematic for the titular heroines. This figuration suggests that their standing as racialized Cuban women—Cecilia as a *mulata* and Cisneros as white—makes them, respectively, either more inherently dangerous or more vulnerable, while simultaneously fashioning them both as victims.
- Finally, although both protagonists are victimized by their respective geopolitical contexts—Cecilia by the corruption produced by slavery and colonialism in Cuba, and Cisneros by Spanish repression and US imperialist exploitation—they are also represented as both actively challenging and being complicit in their emplotments.

In these ways, the oppositions Cecilia and Cisneros are meant to embody are simultaneously manipulated and subverted, giving them a shared agency that not only draws power from, but also breaks their gothicized molds.

---

5. Beidler has noted how Villaverde attributes "much of [Cecilia's] downfall to personal faults associated with her mulata heritage." Beidler, *The Island Called Paradise,* 23.

Because both Villaverde and Cisneros's stories depend upon claims of historicity and factuality, I draw from Hayden White's notion that historical accounts are emplotted "by identifying the kind of story that has been told" in generic terms.[6] In categorizing "romance" as an emplotment mode in chronicles, White notes how historians take disparate accounts and craft them into a "comprehensive or archetypal story form."[7] White's theorizing of a "poetics of history" is helpful in analyzing literary narratives about Cuba, especially those by century's end, which based their claims on their "factual" or "historical" foundations. While Villaverde and Cisneros establish their narratives as "true" accounts, the gothic romance genre is a key element in their emplotment, and, thereby, in their anticolonial political goals. By insisting on the factuality of the gothicized representations that both narratives engage with, Villaverde and Cisneros sought to intervene discursively within the context of the struggle for Cuban independence.

Cecilia Valdés tells the story of a free "mulatta," born of the illicit relationship between a white Spanish merchant and slave trader, Cándido Gamboa, and his also free "mulatta" mistress. Gamboa, who is married to a moneyed white *criolla* with whom he has two daughters and a son, takes the illegitimate newborn away from his mistress. He places the baby in an orphanage where illegitimate children are given the last name Valdés as a way to "whiten" them. After losing her child, the mother goes insane and is interned in a hospital so that the child, Cecilia, is raised by her also "mulatta" grandmother. With little supervision, Cecilia roams the streets of Havana, growing into a strikingly beautiful, strong-headed, and ambitious young woman who plans to marry a white man so that her child can be whiter and they can rise in Cuba's caste-like society. Cecilia sets her sights on Leonardo Gamboa—who is actually her half-brother, though neither one of them knows this—and despite Cándido's efforts to separate them (including imprisoning Cecilia), the two find a way to be together and Cecilia eventually

---

6. White, *Metahistory*, 7.

7. White, *Metahistory*, 8. In White's gendered concept of emplotment, the Romance is "fundamentally a drama of self-identification symbolized by the hero's transcendence of the world of experience, his victory over it, and his final liberation from it—the sort of drama associated with the Grail legend or the story of the resurrection of Christ in Christian mythology. It is a drama of the triumph of good over evil, virtue over vice, of light over darkness, and of the ultimate transcendence of man." White, *Metahistory*, 8–9.

gives birth to a daughter. But Leonardo soon tires of the responsibility and abandons Cecilia to marry his white, upper-class fiancée Isabel. Consumed by a desire for vengeance, Cecilia persuades Pimienta, a free "mulatto"enamored of her, to stop the wedding by killing Isabel. But he murders Leonardo, instead, and slips away unsuspected. The novel ends with Cecilia imprisoned as an accomplice to the murder in the same hospital where her mother is kept, which enables mother and daughter to reunite, before the former dies, her sanity restored. In the novel's brief conclusion, there is no further mention of what happens to Cecilia and her daughter, who is the product of incest produced by the geoculture of slavery in Cuba.

In adding to the significant body of scholarship on Villaverde's 1882 novel, I specifically focus on how he gothicized elements in his heroine's characterization to signify her dangerousness. Further, the novel suggests that Cecilia's menace is directly related to her racial mixture. Vera M. Kutzinski has noted how, historically, anxieties over the emergence of the mixed-race population in Cuba "can be traced back to the fear of slave insurrections that pervaded the first half of the nineteenth century as a result of the successful Haitian Revolution (1791–1803) and to the negrophobic 'Africanization of Cuba' scare brought on by ever-increasing demands for slave labor that accompanied the rapid expansion of Cuba's sugar industry."[8] Specifically with regard to the eponymous protagonist, Humberto López Cruz has observed how "el personaje de Cecilia unifica y destruye, al mismo tiempo, a los personajes centrales de la novela" [she unifies and destroys, at the same time, the central characters of the novel].[9] Along similar lines, Diana Alvarez-Amell has challenged the novel's canonical categorization as a realist "novela costumbrista" [novel of manners], noting how Cecilia embodies "la versión criolla de la mujer fatal o la 'Belle dame sans merci' de la literatura europea" [the creole version of the femme fatale or the beautiful woman without mercy of European literature].[10] Arguing against critical readings that dismiss the novel's "romantic"

---

8. Kutzinski, *Sugar's Secrets*, 5. She has also noted how "the Aponte Conspiracy of 1812 and the conspiracy of La Escalera (The Ladder) of 1844" are specific examples of such insurrections. Kutzinski, *Sugar's Secrets*, 5.

9. López Cruz, "'Cecilia Valdés': La mulatería como símbolo," 52. Translation mine.

10. Alvarez-Amell, "Las dos caras de Cecilia Valdés," 2. Translation mine.

aspects while advocating for its understanding as a "texto literario híbrido" [hybrid literary text], Alvarez-Amell adds that reading Cecilia "como ejemplar de una sociedad no consigue destacar aquello que la distingue, es decir, la extrañeza de este personaje" [as the exemplar of a society fails to highlight that which distinguishes her: namely, the strangeness of her character].[11] My argument here is that it is precisely this "strangeness" that gothicizes Cecilia and constructs Cuba as a gothic geoculture.

Focusing on the gothicized aspects of Villaverde's novel locates the work within a genre that for many Latin American writers and scholars has represented "a foreign fictional mode [rejected] in favor of more local forms of fiction–such as magic realism."[12] In examining the gothic in Latin America, however, Enrique Ajuria Ibarra has called for a more expansive view that "explores [the] Gothic *and* Latin America" to reveal the ways in which the region has been gothicized, and to recognize the gothic "as a mobile catalyst [that] moves narratively, transtextually and transculturally, as it constantly finds rich and fascinating localities that are subject to Othering, mis-recognition and monstrification."[13] Further, in recognizing "the global flow of [the] Gothic," as Ajuria Ibarra suggests, we find that Villaverde's gothicizations fall within what Justin D. Edwards and Sandra Guardini Vasconcelos identify as the gothic's reemergence in the Americas. For Edwards and Guardini Vasconcelos, the gothic adaptations in the region "underscore politically charged ghosts and monsters that return the colonial Other to the center of Empire and foreground the unease and complications of Gothic figures."[14] Given that Villaverde expanded and pub-

---

11. Alvarez-Amell, "Las dos caras de Cecilia Valdés," 6, 7, 9. Translation mine.

12. Ajuria Ibarra, "Exploring Gothic and/in Latin America," 7. Along a similar line, Aldana Reyes notes the difficulty in exploring "the history of the Spanish Gothic [due to] the country's reluctance to use this word to describe national outputs that would, if considered under the paragraphs by which the Gothic is measured in Anglophone countries, be found to be part of the canon in either content or intent." Aldana Reyes, *The Spanish Gothic*, 9.

13. Ajuria Ibarra, "Exploring Gothic and/in Latin America," 7, emphasis in original.

14. Edwards and Guardini Vasconcelos, "Tropicalizing the Gothic," 2. In addition, Casanova-Vizcaíno and Ortiz observe that "the lack of criticism examining Latin American Gothic should not be considered evidence of the absence of this mode in the subcontinent, but rather a testimony of the evolution of literary history and

lished his novel while living in the United States, the story's blend of realist historicity and gothic romance exemplifies the globalized function of the gothic within the geoculture of slavery, contributing to our understanding of the complex and variegated literary flows created by transamericanity during the nineteenth century.[15]

The primacy of the mixed-race or "mulatto" characters in the novel has led scholars to highlight the significance of Villaverde's work in giving this racial group primary roles and voices within Cuban society, signaling their historical rise as a social class in the nineteenth century.[16] Furthermore, William Luis has noted the importance of the fact that, as an antislavery work, the 1882 *Cecilia Valdés* represents the unpunished killing of a white man by a "mulatto." This plot twist, Luis observes, "is a radical departure from the other antislavery novels," especially since Leonardo's death "implies the death of the Gamboa family, [thereby signaling] an end to a historical exploitation of black and mulatto women by white men."[17] In addition to the novel's radical stance in this sense, Villaverde's 1882 revision is significant, as Rodrigo Lazo argues, because it "emerges in part from a network of publishing efforts that develop in the United States during the nineteenth century in response to and in conjunction with Cuban anticolonial politics."[18] Against that background, the novel "engages the hemispheric dimensions of racism, slavery and imperialism." Further, Lazo has observed that "Villaverde's ultimate position against slavery developed in tandem with his view of the United States as a power more interested in its own hemispheric ambitions than in Cuban independence," which led

---

global capitalism." Casanova-Vizcaíno and Ortiz, *Latin American Gothic in Literature and Culture*, 5.

15. In writing about fantastic literature in Latin America, Duncan has noted how "nineteenth-century romanticism ushered in a taste for the bizarre and the uncanny in literature. Interest in ghost stories, strange legends, and tales of the supernatural and inexplicable came from the United States and northern Europe and comfortably settled into Spanish American drawing rooms." Duncan, *Unraveling the Real*, 1.

16. López Cruz notes how "la presencia del mulato confirma el surgimiento de un nuevo elemento social, deviniendo la mulatería como realidad autóctona de la región" [the presence of the mulatto confirms the rise of a new social element, and represents racial mixing as an inherent reality of the region]. López Cruz, "'Cecilia Valdés': La mulatería como símbolo," 55. Translation mine.

17. Luis, "*Cecilia Valdés*," 18.

18. Lazo, "Filibustering Cuba," 3.

him to renounce annexation, denounce the United States, and change his position on slavery, an "evolution that paved the way for a rewriting of *Cecilia Valdés.*"[19]

Building on Lazo's advocacy for recognizing the novel's genesis and significance as transnational—rather than solely national—I focus here on how some of Cecilia's traits echo the gothicized representations of Cuba found in nineteenth-century transamericanity within the context of US empire. This gothicization raises the question of why—when Villaverde dedicated his novel to *las cubanas,* or Cuban women, and when the novel has been widely read as representing the gendered Cuban nation racialized as a *mulata*—Cecilia's characterization connects her unparalleled beauty to malicious inner qualities.[20] This doubleness, one of the representational constants this study has engaged with, is further amplified when Villaverde racializes Cecilia, stating how "one noticed that despite [her] healthy glow there was *too much* ocher in the color of her face," adding that her "blood *was not pure* and it could be stated with assurance that three or four generations back it had been mixed with Ethiopian blood" (13, emphasis mine). This "strange beauty," produced by the excess of African blood, "endowed her with a sort of magic spell, which did not allow one's mind to wander but instead only to admire her and overlook the shortcomings or excesses of her lineage" (13). In personifying Cecilia, Villaverde imbricates race, gender, and nationality to suggest that the mix produced by the geoculture of slavery in Cuba engendered both her striking physicality and her defective character, further implying that they are one and the same. To support this implication, and like other writers in this study, Villaverde draws on gothicized tropes of bewitchment and moral corruption that link Cecilia to Cuba's geoculture.

---

19. Lazo, "Filibustering Cuba," 3. Lazo, *Writing to Cuba,* 177. Along similar lines, calling the text a "panoramic drama of evil," Beidler has observed that the 1882 edition was "composed by the author after decades of expatriation" in New York and "probably begun in 1879 but not published in Cuba until 1903," or only after Spanish colonial domination had ended. Beidler, *The Island Called Paradise,* 18.

20. For a selection of discussions on the significance of Cecilia as *mulata,* see Beidler chapter on the novel, Kutsinski's introduction, Alvarez-Amell, "*Las dos caras de Cecilia Valdés,*" Gelpí "*El discurso jerárquico,*" Lasarte Varcárcel, "*Nación por caridad,*" Luis, "*Cecilia Valdés,*" López Cruz, "'Cecilia Valdés': La mulatería como símbolo," and Méndez Rodenas, "Tropics of Deceit," among others.

In gothically emplotting his heroine as embodying a troubling doubleness between her angelic beauty and her spiritual malice, Villaverde builds on but also rewrites the trope of the "tragic mulatta." When Cecilia is introduced to the reader in the second chapter—after we have seen her raving mother and cruel father in the similarly gothicized first chapter—the narrator notes:

> A pesar de aquella vida y de aquel traje, parecía tan pura y linda, que estaba uno tentado a creer que jamás dejaría de ser lo que era: cándida niña en cabello que se preparaba a entrar en el mundo por una puerta al parecer de oro, y que vivía sin tener sospecha siquiera de su existencia. (12)

> Despite the life she had led and despite her attire, she seemed so pretty and so pure that a person was tempted to believe that she would never cease to be what she was: an innocent young maiden who was preparing to enter the world through a seemingly golden door, and who spent her days without even suspecting its existence. (14)

Here Villaverde constructs Cecilia as a study in contrasts, as her garments and the evidence of her lived experience contradict her physical characteristics, presenting a puzzle to the observer. The idea that a person looking at Cecilia would disregard the evidence before them to believe in her innocence suggests not only that Cecilia embodies the clash between the performance of purity and the actuality of its opposite, but also that she has the power to persuade others to ignore the obvious.

To this idea that Cecilia's nature is inherently corrupt, the narrator adds the notion that her background—the nurtured part—has also molded her in corrupted ways. Her "school," the narrator adds, was

> las calles de la ciudad, las plazas, los establecimientos públicos, [...], y en tales sitios, según es de presumir, su tierno corazón, formado acaso para dar abrigo a las virtudes que son el más bello encanto de las mujeres, bebió a torrentes las aguas empozoñadas del vicio, se nutrió desde temprano con las escenas de impudicia que ofrece diariamente un pueblo soez y desmoralizado. (12)

the streets of the city, the squares, the public establishments, [. . .], and in such places, one may surmise, her tender heart, meant perhaps to harbor virtues, the loveliest of feminine charms, drank instead in torrents the poisoned waters of vice, and nourished itself from her earliest years on the lewd scenes staged each day by an indecent and depraved people. (14)

By noting that "perhaps" Cecilia's heart would have harbored virtuosity, the narrator introduces doubt that this would have been the case, and the image of her actively imbibing and being strengthened by the "lewd" vices to which she is exposed situates Cecilia as a complicit participant in the geoculture of slavery. This suggestion is further supported by the narrator's next statement that too early in Cecilia's life "the legion of passions that consume the heart and humble the proudest brows knocked on her door" (14). The melodramatic and gothicized language—personifying evil with the agency to summon her—emplots Cecilia into a narrative structure that, in a racialized and gendered narrative universe, foreshadows a tragic ending.

In this way, Cecilia's representation follows the ontological lines of the "tragic mulatta," whose fate, as Eve Allegra Raimon has observed, "depends upon her female gender," given that the sexual vulnerability of the light-skinned female slave "is essential to propel the plot forward and to generate the reader's sympathy and outrage." Further, Raimon notes that "even as the 'white blood' coursing through the veins of a male light-skinned bondman afforded him greater intelligence and subjectivity in period literature, his female counterpart was deployed simultaneously to demonstrate the destructive potential of the slave system to such a heroine's very survival."[21] Within the geocultural frame of Villaverde's novel, Cecilia may not be a slave but she is still shackled both by the racialized cultural norms of her time, which made it impossible for her to marry a white man, and by the suggestion that racial mixture engenders her corrupted character.[22] Indeed, the narrator implies that Cecilia does not help herself by "imbibing" the culture

---

21. Raimon, *The "Tragic Mulatta" Revisited*, 5–6.

22. Guevara proposes: "The image of the eroticized mythic mulata is the creation of a white imaginary eager to contain racial anxieties in a troubled colonial context that simultaneously sought to construct a national identity and to resolve Cuba's race problem." Guevara, "Inexacting Whiteness," 106.

around her and adapting to the structures of power that defined racial castes in Cuba. Villaverde thereby sets up Cecilia as a tragic figure who cannot escape the outcome already determined by the geoculture of slavery in Cuba.

This early representation of Cecilia foreshadows her actions at the novel's end, when upon finding out about the wedding between Leonardo and Isabel, the narrator states that he is not equal to "the task of depicting the tumult of passions that the news gave rise to in the breast of the proud and vengeful mulatta" (489–90). But when the narrator adds that "suffice it to say that in point of fact the lamb turned into a lion," this transformation is not actually surprising since the novel has already suggested that Cecilia really has been a wolf in sheep's clothing all along (491). When Pimienta shows up, unbidden, Cecilia asks what "good angel" has brought him to her, and he replies: "Because my heart told me that Celia [Cecilia] might need me" (490). However, the scene suggests that the influence Cecilia has on Pimienta is not angelic but actually demonic, since she tells him that he must stop the marriage, insinuating that he must do so through violence, and he agrees to comply with her mandate. Juan Gelpí notes that the ending's foreshadowing at the novel's beginning proposes "un claro determinismo que se cifra en la fisonomía" [a clear determinism based on physiognomy]," which is part of what he identifies as "una tensión entre el ser y el parecer" [a tension between being and seeming] in Cecilia's characterization.[23] This duality, racialized as ontological by Villaverde, sets Cecilia on the path to self-destruction.

But while Villaverde emplots Cecilia into the "tragic mulatta" role, the story still spares her and her daughter, the product of an incestuous relationship and thereby understood to be biologically and morally tainted. This reprieve comes even after Cecilia manipulates Pimienta, the free "mulatto" she had rejected because she wanted a white lover, into a murderous rage. However, the geoculture of slavery that constructs the novel's racial and gendered hierarchies foils Cecilia's plan because Pimienta, as a man of mixed race, takes aim against his white rival, Leonardo, rather than against the innocent Isabel. Thereby, the novel sets up the "mulatto" as Cecilia's avenger against the white seducer, but also gives Pimienta's violent assertion of masculinity pri-

---

23. Gelpí, "El discurso jerárquico," 54, 55. Translation mine.

macy over Cecilia's wishes that Leonardo should be spared. While Pimienta's actions frustrate her goals, the fact that he escapes unseen into the crowd and that Cecilia is only temporarily imprisoned leaves an open future for both characters. This futurity is denied to the white characters, whether slave-owning, like the Gamboas (who lose their one male heir), or even those with antislavery sympathies, like Isabel (who joins a convent), thereby challenging the very determinism implied by Pimienta and Cecilia's representations as "tragic" mixed-race characters.[24]

Cecilia is not a "tragic mulatta" in the traditional sense because she is gothicized in ways that complicate how her character is signified. In recognizing that complexity, Sybille Fischer, editor of the novel's English translation, asks whether Villaverde's novel inaugurates "the idea of 'la Cuba mulata,' the idea of a Cuban national identity grounded in miscegenation, or does it, on the contrary, offer new justifications for racial hierarchies?"[25] My response to Fischer's question is that Cecilia's characterization does both: it establishes an idea of Cuban identity by drawing on (and gothicizing) the consequences of a society ruled by racial castes within the geoculture of slavery. In complicating Villaverde's claim that his novel sought to be realist, as opposed to a romance in generic terms, Fischer underscores "the melodramatic aspects of the story," most centrally the trope of incest suggested by the relationship between Cecilia and Leonardo, who share the same father. Citing early and contemporary critics who addressed the novel's reification of racialized power structures, Fischer reads the narrative's conflation of slavery, miscegenation, and incest as proposing "a fictional scenario in which the only real alternative to the colonial slaveholding system—racial equality—remains veiled through narratives that refer us back to the horror and desire forever attached to the idea of incest."[26] That is, Fischer notes how the very notion of racial equality "turns into a possibly transgressive sameness," suggesting why we can

---

24. Buscaglia-Salgado has argued that "the mulatto always moves beyond, not by being *alter* but by being *ultra*. Indeed, in a curious antidote to conquest and reduction, the mulatto subject describes a movement of reverse colonization of the Ideal that is always more, not less, always additive and forever seemingly shifting. The mulatto subject is the true *plus ultra* of the Atlantic world." Buscaglia-Salgado, *Undoing Empire*, xvii.

25. Fischer, "Introduction," xii.

26. Fischer, "Introduction," xxiii.

read Villaverde's representation of Cecilia and other mixed-race characters as embodying an ambivalence that both recognized and feared their power/empowerment in Cuba.²⁷

By suggesting that the island's future is in the hands of troubled (and troubling) mixed-race characters, such as Cecilia and Pimienta, Villaverde's novel warns against the effects of the geoculture of slavery. For one, as Gelpí has noted, "la cuchillada del mulato Pimienta refuerza también la visión de los mulatos y los negros como seres peligrosos e incontenibles que figura en *Cecilia Valdés*" [the stabbing by the mulatto Pimienta also reinforces the vision of mulattos and blacks as dangerous and uncontainable characters, which is found in *Cecilia Valdés*], a representation that Gelpí links to the "visión paranoica de los mulatos y los negros" [paranoid vision of mulattos and blacks] that was prevalent in nineteenth-century Cuban society.²⁸ Along these lines, Gelpí also observes how Cecilia's characterization "no difiere, en lo fundamental, de la que se emplea al presentar a otros personajes negros y mulatos: para el narrador ella también será 'peligrosa'" [does not fundamentally differ from what (Villaverde) employs in presenting other black and mulatto characters: for the narrator she also will be 'dangerous'].²⁹ Because the representation of slavery in the Cuban context, as Lazo has pointed out, stood both for itself as a system of racial oppression and as a metaphor for the colonial—or enslaved—status of Cuba, the gothicized elements in Villaverde's novel argue against both slavery and colonialism (whether from Spain or the United States).³⁰ Moreover, Cecilia's survival in a narrative in which she has caused nearly everyone else's downfall challenges her emplotment as a tragic figure so that, even if her ending is not promising, she is spared the ultimate tragedy—her own (and/or her daughter's) death.

---

27. Fischer, "Introduction," xxiii.
28. Gelpí, "El discurso jerárquico," 53. Translation mine.
29. Gelpí, "El discurso jerárquico," 54. Translation mine. In addition, Lasarte Varcárcel has further queried whether the novel can promote "un discurso racista y jerárquico a la vez que abierto y tolerante, promotor al menos de la coexistencia pacífica si es que no de un cierto tipo de mestizaje limitado y contradictorio" [a racist and hierarchical discourse that is also open and tolerant, promoting at least pacific coexistence if not a certain type of limited and contradictory racial mixing]. Lasarte Varcárcel, "Nación por caridad," 23. Translation mine.
30. Lazo, "Filibustering Cuba," 21.

In my reading, the melodramatic aspects of Villaverde's story depend on the gothicized emplotment of his racially mixed heroine as embodying troubling aspects of Cuban identity. Beidler has observed that Villaverde "fashioned a complex seduction plot and then wedded it to the dark psychosexual mysteries of popular gothic sensationalism," relying on a "conflicted narrator [who] can simultaneously adore Cecilia yet attribute much of her downfall to personal faults associated with her mulata heritage."[31] This duality in Cecilia, and in the narrator's own attitude toward her, allows Villaverde's novel to function as an antislavery and nationally foundational narrative that simultaneously draws on gothicized tropes to caution against the influence of Cuba's geoculture by reinforcing racist notions about the dangers of racial mixing. In that way, the novel articulates anxieties about the destructive (especially self-destructive) consequences of colonialism and slavery, and the imbrications of race, gender, and nationality that they produced.

In embodying this cautionary tale, Cecilia functions as a negative double of Cisneros, whose later narrative must be framed within its geopolitical moment—the actual emergence of US empire in the hemisphere. Louis A. Pérez, Jr. has argued that this development was accompanied by "a master narrative that propounded unabashedly a stance of moral superiority: Americans given to selfless service to mankind, without ulterior motive, without selfish intent." Through US involvement in Cuba, "Americans [. . .] assigned themselves the role of moral force in defense of those inalienable rights with which they had invented themselves."[32] This "duty of destiny" was disseminated through many forms, including literary and nonliterary texts, so that Cuba—embroiled in its own pro-independence insurgency against Spain—became a launching pad for overseas US imperialism.[33] In 1898, winning its war against Spain established the United States as an empire on the rise in the Pacific and the Americas, forever changing the global geopolitical map.

Within this context, and little more than a decade after the publication of Villaverde's novel, "the vernacular of empire" on Cuba shapeshifted away from the gothic specters that had been conjured to warn against the potential dangers inherent to the island's geocul-

---

31. Beidler, *The Island Called Paradise*, 23, 24.
32. Pérez, *Cuba in the American Imagination*, 7.
33. Pérez, *Cuba in the American Imagination*, 7.

ture.³⁴ Instead, gothicized images of emaciated corpses, of women starved, shackled, or about to be murdered, were widely disseminated to unambiguously advocate for US imperial expansion into Cuba. In his historical work on such representations, Pérez notes that the island "underwent anthropomorphic transformation" so that a "new metaphor of Cuba emerged, one that imagined Cuba as a woman and depicted the island as a victim, mostly the victim of the misdeeds of Spanish men."³⁵ Pérez argues that these end-of-century representations served to promote "notions of chivalric duty from which to infer gender-scripted obligations and culturally derived codes of conduct to act upon," all in the service of empire.³⁶ Indeed, by century's end, representations of Cuba as a woman in need of rescue were mainly aimed at US white women so they could help persuade the larger US public that they should "provide protection to women or to a country—emblematically feminized—that rival men [were] violating."³⁷ Though, as this study shows, the gendering of Cuba as a woman was not new to 1898, the figuration of the island "in plaintive pose beseeching the Americans for rescue and redemption" signaled a change in the gothicized rhetoric on Cuba within transamericanity.

This representational shift in transforming Cuba from femme fatale to damsel in distress depended on hyper-negative and racialized portrayals of Spain. María DeGuzmán has argued that "in what has been designated the Spanish-American War, [. . .] Spain functioned as both historical and symbolic contestant in the formation of Anglo-American national identity with imperial ambitions."³⁸ Advocating for the term "Spanish-Cuban-American War" as "more historically accurate," DeGuzmán shows how "Anglo-American imperial identity was forged in distinct counterpoint to images of Spain and Spaniards."³⁹ Along these lines, in Cisneros's story, Spain and Spaniards are cast as gothic villains who cause her travails, including a threat to her sexual "purity,"

---

34. Pérez notes that the "metaphorical motifs" used by the United States to represent Cuba were not "necessarily original or unique" in "the history of colonial narratives," which he describes as "the vernacular of empire." Pérez, *Cuba in the American Imagination*, 3.
35. Pérez, *Cuba in the American Imagination*, 71.
36. Pérez, *Cuba in the American Imagination*, 71.
37. Pérez, *Cuba in the American Imagination*, 73.
38. DeGuzmán, *Spain's Long Shadow*, 139.
39. DeGuzmán, *Spain's Long Shadow*, 139.

and her imprisonment until she is rescued by the United States. Thereby, Cisneros's text captures the moment and manner in which Cuba transitioned discursively from a gothicized corruptive influence to a threatened gothic victim.[40]

In response to this ideological shift, the mode of dissemination also changed. Figurations of Cuba as victim were not promoted mainly through fictionalized narratives, or travelogues, as in the texts I have previously examined. Instead, these portrayals were commonly found in journalistic reports, as well as in newspaper cartoons and illustrations, giving such signifiers a greater sense of factuality and immediacy than fictionalized representations and travelogues. Cisneros's text is dedicated "To the Women of America," and is framed by an introduction penned by Julian Hawthorne, followed by the "Protests and Petitions" on behalf of Cisneros (including one to the Pope by Julia Ward Howe, whose work on Cuba I mention in chapters 1 and 2). Next is an account of the events from the perspective of Karl Decker, the reporter sent to Cuba by William Randolph Hearst to rescue Cisneros. Only after Decker's narrative ends does Cisneros get to tell "Her Own Story," which is then followed by a summary "History of Cuba" and a "Chronology." As Elizabeth Lowry remarks, of the book's more than two-hundred pages, Cisneros's autobiographical story takes up "less than half of the book."[41] The masculine-focused framing of Cisneros's tale demonstrates what Lowry argues is the "control" that Hearst wanted to exercise over the narrative, a control that was compounded through photographs and illustrations included in the paratext. All of this was done in the service of emplotting Cisneros as a gothic heroine, thereby setting up the carefully crafted elements of the book as the factual narrative.

Sensationalism and "yellow journalism" were also significant to the mode through which predominant representations of Cuba were circulated by century's end. David B. Sachsman and David W. Bulla argue that, within the context of booming newspaper readership, "the sensa-

---

40. Pérez notes how by 1898 Cuba was figured in US media as a woman "fashioned as a supplicant appealing to the Americans for intercession in behalf of her well-being." The United States thereby "politicized the language; more precisely, they fashioned a vernacular perfectly suited to the moral imperative with which they embarked on empire." Pérez, *Cuba in the American Imagination*, 87, 89.

41. Lowry, "The Flower of Cuba," 180.

tional became a commodity in the middle of the nineteenth century," and "moved into override" after the US Civil War.[42] Yellow journalism, they add, "was not just about the visible traits of large headlines, out-of-control rhetoric, and seedy news topics," it was also about Hearst, Joseph Pulitzer, and other men "driven by social and political causes."[43] Within this context, Carol Wilcox notes how by 1897 "newspaper readership was at one of its highest points in [US] history," adding that "the circulation of [Hearst's] *Journal* and Pulitzer's rival paper, the *New York World*, stood at 700,000 and 800,000, respectively."[44] In addition, many Cuban "revolutionary publishers set up presses in New York rather than attempt to publish at home because of the hardships brought about by Spain's occupation of the island." In the case of Cisneros, she had been imprisoned for more than year before US newspapers "discovered her plight in August 1897." Once that happened, Hearst and Pulitzer competed fiercely to cover her story, with the *Journal* publishing "more than 250 items about Evangelina."[45] In turn, such coverage caught the attention of the US government, leading to a discussion of the "Cisneros Affair" by President William McKinley's cabinet.[46] Cisneros's story riveted the US public only four months before the *Maine* mysteriously sank in Havana harbor in February 1898, igniting the Spanish-American War. In these ways, Cisneros's account is very much steeped in the politics of empire at century's end, and within the yellow journalism that aided and abetted the US pursuit of imperial power in the Americas.

As a participant in this tradition of sensationalist journalism, and in crafting the narrative structure of his introduction, Hawthorne—the son of a nineteenth-century US literary scion—invests himself with the authorial expertise to legitimize her narrative as a significant literary artifact. To do this, he points out that while he will not be the one to tell the story, given that "it is told by the protagonists as only they could do it," the narrative itself, "in its dramatis personae, in its dash, intrigue, and cumulative interest," is "ideally perfect" because the "desirable components [of a good story] are all present" (18). Argu-

---

42. Sachsman and Bulla, *Sensationalism*, xxiv, xxv.
43. Sachsman and Bulla, *Sensationalism*, xxvi.
44. Wilcox, "Cuba's 'Hot Little Rebel,'" 156.
45. Wilcox, "Cuba's 'Hot Little Rebel,'" 156–57.
46. Wilcox, "Cuba's 'Hot Little Rebel,'" 165.

ing for the understanding of Cisneros's story in terms of genre, Hawthorne carefully identifies the elements that make the story so gripping because of its seemingly fictitious elements. Hawthorne writes:

> A tropic island, embosomed in azure seas off the coast of the Spanish Main; a cruel war, waged by the minions of despotism against the spirit of patriotism and liberty; a beautiful maiden, risking all for her country, captured, insulted, persecuted, and cast into a loathsome dungeon. (19)

Hawthorne lists the generic components of a gothic romance—time, location, victim, villain—and sets up the "embosomed" island and the imprisoned maiden as parallels to each other in opposition to the despot who assails them, representing Spain as waging war against the ideals of "patriotism and liberty" identified with the United States (19). Through this rhetorical conflation, both the island and the maiden are represented as being on the US side of the conflict.

In portraying Cisneros as an embodiment of Cuba, Hawthorne draws a sharp distinction between innocence and wickedness, beauty and ugliness, lovability and hatefulness, and calls to mind "the old Romances," which he notes leave no room for ambivalence or ambiguity. Cisneros, Hawthorne argues, is the perfect Romantic heroine because

> none could be more innocent, constant and adorable than she; none more wicked detestable and craven than her enemies. All is right and lovable on the one side, all ugly and hateful on the other. As in the old Romances, there is no uncertainty as to which way our sympathies should turn. The opposition is as clean and clear as between black and white. (19)

Hawthorne's use of the adjective "wicked" here contrasts sharply with the way Villaverde uses it when describing Cecilia. While Villaverde describes his heroine as embodying wickedness, Hawthorne represents Spain as evil. Articulating the conflict between Spain and Cisneros/Cuba as "between black and white," Hawthorne not only racializes Spain as he whitens Cisneros/Cuba, but he also entirely dismisses the possibility of racial mixing, arguably the source of greatest anxiety in

Villaverde's novel. In that way, we see how, by century's end, imperial ambition had superseded the racial anxieties that permeated many of the earlier texts in this study.

Building on this idea that the narrative structure determines the ending, Hawthorne categorizes the newspaper's decision to intervene in Cisneros's fate as like "that of some puissant prince of fairy legend, despatching a courteous but cogent message to the Ogre, calling his attention to the wrong done his captive, and demanding justice on her behalf" (20). Personified as the fated rescuer, the US newspaper becomes the heroic figure who not only makes demands on behalf of the captive Cisneros, but also issues those demands in "the names of womanhood of America and England" (20). Like Villaverde's novel, where Cecilia stands for Cuban womanhood, Hawthorne portrays Cisneros as a signifier for white womanhood with a transamerican and even transatlantic reach.

Further, Cisneros's whiteness is equated with that of US and British women, all of whom are racially counterpoised against the unreasonable Spanish "Ogre" as their polar opposite. Because the Spanish monster, however, "had made up his mind to torture and devour his victim in the wicked old ogreish way, and was not to be diverted from his purpose by any consideration of civilized humanity" (19–20), Hawthorne argues that intervention became unavoidable. He easily crafts, by drawing from gothic and other fantastical fear-inducing narratives such as fairy tales, an emplotment that argues for the rescue of the maiden by the United States as a cultural imperative.

Giving away the story's resolution, Hawthorne assures his readers that they are in for a "real" fairy tale, even up to the happy ending. With nearly cinematic style, Hawthorne goes on to describe how, although the venture is not immediately successful, "the miracle takes place; the Ogre is defrauded; the maiden is rescued," and he returns to the connection between factuality and fiction by noting: "No fairy princess could be more lovely than this fairy-like little Cuban maiden: her features have the delicate refinement only given by race," adding that Cisneros is "a heroine worth daring an army of Ogres for, even for her own sake" (25, 26). Cisneros's beauty, which Hawthorne racializes as white, implicitly makes her a worthy "cause," though there is, of course, also Cuba to consider. Thus, he concludes: "In the person of Evangelina Cisneros, Cuba appeals to us. With what grace can we receive the one and repel the other?" (27). In becoming the gothic heroine of the tale Hawthorne tells, Cisneros is emplotted, as Pérez suggests in his own analysis, as a stand-in for Cuba, leading Hawthorne to issue a direct imperialist appeal to his readers for US intervention.

Unlike the fictionalized texts I have examined, Hawthorne's claims of factuality repurpose the gothic, using its tropes not as a warning about coloniality or the geoculture of slavery in Cuba, but as justification for it. Hawthorne claims that Cisneros's story was "also more romantic" than real life and, thereby, "more in the fashion of the Arabian Nights and the Gothic fairy-tales of Medieval ages" (17). By categorizing Cisneros's story within the gothic's inception in Europe, Hawthorne associates the genre more with escapism than with political concerns.[47] In combining the Orientalist exoticism of the "Arabian Nights" with "fairy-tales," Hawthorne attempts to disconnect the gothic from the racial hauntings of its hemispheric context by making it seem more global in its justification of colonial intervention. To that end, Hawthorne emplots Cisneros's story through romantic and sentimental tropes to make the story's factuality more spectacular, and he underlines the seemingly implausible elements of the tale—its gothicized characteristics—to strengthen rather than destabilize dominant racial and gender ideologies in the service of the US imperial project.

Ultimately, in Hawthorne's "Introduction" we find none of the gothic doublings, specters, and fears of corruption raised by other writers—including Villaverde—in some of the representations of Cuba produced within the sixty-year period of this study. Also absent from Hawthorne's representation of Cisneros as Cuba is any mention of the geoculture of slavery and its transamericanity, or of its legacy, as well as any ambivalence or ambiguity about the resulting imbrications of race, gender, and nation. On the contrary, Hawthorne's "Introduction" is a paean to US imperialism, one that draws on the gothic and the "Black Legend" not to mediate fears of Cuba's dangerous geoculture, but as a rallying cry to unify all US Americans in the pursuit of empire. By century's end, as Cuba metamorphosed from gothicized monster into

---

47. Edwards explains that scholars have identified the difference between American and European gothic traditions as being between literature "often dismissed as escapist romantic nonsense" and the American gothic's engagement with "self-reflection [. . .] from its own position as a voice of the marginal: women, gays, people of color, Americans." Edwards, *Gothic Passages,* xx-xxi.

gothic heroine—and as concerns over the geoculture of slavery ceased to be an overt political issue after abolition both in the United States and on the island—so did the genre shapeshift from a rhetorical articulation about fears of self-destruction into a justification and support for US imperial expansion.

While Cisneros is initially emplotted by Hawthorne as a gothic heroine, and while she also draws on these tropes to represent herself, when she finally gets to write her own tale she also adds elements that challenge such representations. For one, Cisneros represents herself as complicit in plotting against Spain during the violent rebellion that had begun in 1895. When her father is arrested with the "papers which gave into [Spanish authorities'] hands the whole plot of our rising," Cisneros uses the pronoun "our" to signal that she was part of the revolutionary plot, and to take ownership of her own complicity, highlighting her agency in doing so (132). At the same time, and in emplotting her own story, Cisneros casts the new Spanish Governor of the Isle of Pines, Col. José Bérriz, as the villain of her narrative. Noting that Bérriz had been described as "a coward" for having himself named governor of the island prison "so he would not have to go into battle and fight," Cisneros adds, "Had he not been a coward he would not have acted as he did. Brave men do not attack girls, who do not carry swords and cannot defend themselves" (156). Unlike her previous self-representations as a brave rebel woman, who was raised by her father as a "soldier's daughter," here Cisneros portrays herself as an inoffensive and defenseless "girl." In this way, Cisneros is complicit with the emplotment of her story as a gothic romance, one in which the villain and victim are clearly identifiable, but she still maintains narrative control of when and why she draws on the genre for her own political purposes.

Indeed, Cisneros soon subverts this self-representation as a defenseless "girl" by noting how she was armed and planned to use her weapon either on Bérriz or on herself, because death was preferable to dishonor. Cisneros narrates how after telling her father of Bérriz's unwanted sexual advances, he "said that I must always carry my dagger and that it was not hard to die, and that if I died I should see my mother and he would come to us there" (165). Cisneros tells how, as feared by her father, the Spanish colonel shows up at her door in full military regalia with the apparent purpose of seducing her. While she stalls in opening the door, he breaks it down and begins to profess his love to her, noting that he had the power to free her father, and that "if you really wished to serve your father and gain his liberty you would be kinder to me [. . .]. You cannot expect to have all favors and give nothing in return" (170). He suggests that what she needs to give him is her sexual favors, but as he gets ready to assault her and she tries to escape him, a group of Cuban men storm in and stop Bérriz (172). Though Cisneros is saved by the men who intervene, she gives readers a clear indication that she was not going to submit without a fight to the death. Indeed, historical records suggest that Cisneros may have invited Bérriz to her lodgings so that he would be ambushed.[48] That Cisneros omits the possibility that she could have been sexual bait in the planned attack on the Spanish officer shows how she allows herself to be emplotted as a potential victim rather than represent herself as a femme fatale. This latter self-representation would have made her much less appealing to a US audience eager to feel like heroic saviors in a classic melodrama.

The attack on Bérriz results in Cisneros's arrest and imprisonment in Havana at the "Recojidas [. . .] prison for abandoned women in Cuba"—the same prison in which Cecilia is placed by Gamboa to prevent her and Leonardo from being together—where Cisneros draws the most gothicized representations of her plight as an emplotted heroine (183). In crafting herself again as a victim, Cisneros paints a racialized picture that separates her, as a white Cuban woman, from the other women imprisoned in the jail. Cisneros states: "We had lived among prisoners and among soldiers, but we had never met the awful creatures who were locked up in that jail which was to be my home for fifteen months" (183). Here she draws a distinction between the men she had lived among, without fear for herself, and the "awful creatures," or the women imprisoned there, whom she represents as subhuman.

Cisneros builds on the gothicized environment by noting how she and her sister, Carmen, "found ourselves in a great cage with, it seemed to me, hundreds of the most terrible women that could be dreamed of" (184). By describing this moment as nightmarish, Cisneros seeks to make her experience intelligible to her US readers: the fear she felt went beyond anything connected to the real. Cisneros describes how

---

48. Prados-Torreira, *Mambisas*, 138.

she and her sister, "tried to find a corner where we would be alone, but they followed us and made fun of our terror" (184). The scene establishes a sense of danger for Cisneros and her sister, as white Cuban women, to spend time "with all these negresses and evil white women, who had been taken from the streets for committing robbery and murder" (185). The racial and class contrasts here give these passages their strongest gothicized tone, in that they whiten Cisneros and position her and her sister as imperiled by the noxious influence of the other women in the prison.

In layering on the gothic sense created by this prison and by the company of these "evil" black and white women, Cisneros states boldly:

> I would rather be dead and in my grave, with the cross at my head and a stone at my feet, than to be for one day in that place again. It was not the day that made me wish to die. In the daytime we huddled all together like scared sheep; the negresses, the women who never talked to me, and I. We were in a pen, like a pen for wild animals. (186)

The idea that she would prefer death to returning to the jail, and that, during the day, the women all behaved and were treated like animals, is meant to add fuel to the indignation that she wanted her US women readers to feel as she recounted her story. She is not only being animalized by her situation, but her purity—physical and spiritual—is being threatened by the conditions in which she has been placed by Spanish officials.

Further, it is through the narrative of her imprisonment that Cisneros develops the notion that she was being corrupted by the place and purpose of the jail. In one of the most surprising passages, because of how she represents the violence of her feelings, Cisneros notes:

> The negresses were kind enough to me after awhile, but they could not see why I turned my back when people came in and looked at us; one of them took me by the shoulder one day and pulled me around with my face to the bars, and said, 'Get used to it; you might as well begin now,' and then they all laughed, and a ragged man held up a little boy to look in and see, and the little boy laughed and put his

hands over his eyes to mock me. If I had had a machete there I would have killed that woman. Being in prison does not make one feel like being good. (187)

Once more, Cisneros highlights the racial and class distinction between herself and the other women prisoners since they do not care about or understand the principle of privacy and the impropriety of a white woman being ogled in public (the prison's bars faced the street so that the prisoners were constantly on display). The virulence with which Cisneros tells of how she would have killed the woman who mocked her provides a sense of how the prison atmosphere corrupts and prevents her from feeling "like being good." In this story, Cisneros effectively emplots herself as a gothic victim of Spain, one who is brought into contact with contaminating racial and class "Others" who threaten to blight her. She thus represents herself in ways that make her clearly intelligible to her white US audience, which would have likely sympathized with her despair at being among these racially and socially abject women.

Shortly after this turning point, Cisneros describes how plans for her rescue began, noting how identification between her and white US women was key to this effort. She tells of how the prison warden first tells her that the *New York Journal* was following her case, and then a correspondent from that newspaper visited her in prison. She notes how "he told me he was a correspondent of the New York Journal, [and] that the paper he represented had heard of my case and was endeavoring to have me released" (189). After she is transferred to another part of the prison with other women political prisoners, she is also told that "American women were trying to help me" (190). But then Cisneros notes how all visitors are forbidden to her after "the Queen Regent of Spain had cabled [the Spanish Captain General in Cuba] in response to the petitions of the American ladies and had ordered me to be placed incommunicado" (195). Eventually, she receives a letter from Decker, asking her if she can figure out how to escape. She designs her own escape plan and helps her rescuers successfully enact it so that she soon finds herself free, and in a safe house. In that place, she is given "a suit of boy's clothes, and told [that] I must put them on. I was afraid I should have to cut my hair [but] I got some pomade and plastered my hair down very smooth" (207). She concludes this passage by noting: "All the way across Havana I walked with long steps, with a cigar in my mouth" (208). This scene, which gives the reader the sense that Cisneros only performed masculinity to obtain her freedom, also reassures readers that she retained her long hair, an important signifier of her femininity. Further, the scene also suggests that Cisneros was very much aware of how and when to show feminine vulnerability.

Ultimately, despite attempts to control Cisneros's narrative by encapsulating it within masculine frames, the text as a whole reflects a clear tension between Cisneros's representation as a victim by both Hawthorne and Decker, and her own self-representation both as a defenseless girl and as a courageous woman who was no damsel in distress. Lowry notes that "it is clear that the woman the American Establishment expected Evangelina to be and the woman she had to be in order to survive were fundamentally at odds" (188). Further, what that narrative dichotomy shows within this project is that while US representations of Cuba by century's end depended on the "victim's" emplotment in the service of imperialist expansion, Cisneros—who became and also saw herself as representative of Cuba—wrote purposefully to challenge and contradict that narrative while simultaneously adopting such emplotment in the moments when it served her political purposes.[49]

Although her story is emplotted as that of the typical gothic heroine—a persecuted "virgin" fleeing moral corruption from a villain or monster—Cisneros repeatedly highlights the ways in which she was raised in masculinized terms that subvert the reductive gendered conventions of the gothic romance.[50] Early in her narrative, Cisneros

---

49. Under McKinley's presidency, in 1898, the United States acquired Cuba, Puerto Rico, the Philippines, and Hawai'i. While Cisneros may have had great hopes—as many other Cubans did—that Cuba would be given full independence by the United States, it was not to be. After the US intervention in Cuba, the island was occupied by US forces from 1898 to 1902, when Cuba was proclaimed as a republic but was then exposed to a thorough process of "Americanization." Utset, *A Cultural History of Cuba*. After the invasion, Cuba was ruled under the Platt Amendment (1902–1934), which gave the United States plenary power to invade the island at will. Pérez, *Cuba under the Platt Amendment*.

50. For a discussion on the gothic heroine trope, see Ellis, "Can You Forgive Her?," 457–68. Winter also has noted how in female gothic texts, "the main task of

describes how her "father was a strange man in some ways," who used to tell her that "it seems to me that you should have been my son and not my daughter" (126). In noting her father's strangeness, partly to explain why she was perceived as exceptional by US readers, Cisneros adds that "my father treated me more like a son" (125). She states that her father discussed his work with her, as well as politics, telling her stories about the Ten Years' War against Spain (1868–1878), in which he fought. By noting how her father did not treat her "as most Cuban fathers treat their daughters," and how he taught her "something more of the world than most Cuban girls [. . .] ever dream of knowing," Cisneros appropriates masculine-identified traits of political savvy that contest her casting as gothic heroine (126, 129). This is one way in which Cisneros challenges her emplotment, thereby inserting an implicit tension into her representation.

Cisneros's autobiographical narrative and Villaverde's novel appear to represent two seemingly opposing ways in which gothic tropes of moral corruption and feminine victimhood were associated with Cuba by century's end. But while Villaverde and Cisneros's narratives differ in their use of these tropes—the first gothicizes its heroine as morally corrupt because she is racially mixed, while the latter is racialized as "white" to represent her as a gothic victim/heroine in danger of being corrupted by Spain—they both share in their figurations as victims of their geopolitical context. For Villaverde's protagonist, the geoculture of slavery enables her incestuous relationship with her half-brother, Leonardo, while also foiling her murderous plot against her white upper-class rival on the day of Leonardo's wedding. Cisneros, for her part, is complicit in but also resists her representation as a persecuted maiden in need of rescue by the United States as a way to advocate for action against Spanish colonialism in Cuba.

Because of their historical context, both narratives exemplify the ways in which gothicized tropes were influenced by the geopolitics of their time. Rodrigo Lazo has eloquently argued for an understanding of the influence on Villaverde of his time in the United States so that his "novel represented not only a resistance to the Spanish empire and its lengthy hold on Cuba but also a refusal to be swallowed and for-

---

the Gothic heroine is to uncover and name the horrors that fill her world." Winter, *Subjects of Slavery*, 12.

gotten within the entrails of the other empire [a reference to Cuban patriot José Martí's depiction of his life in the United States], the one in which he lived for more than half of his life."[51] In historicizing Cisneros's narrative, Carol Wilcox has pointed to how "Evangelina escaped only twenty-three weeks before the sinking of the *Maine* in Havana harbor," the event that triggered the war between Spain and the United States in 1898. Further, Wilcox observes, the *Journal*'s coverage of her case "may have tipped public sentiment in the United States toward war with Spain" that year.[52] Juxtaposing these narratives reveals how gothic tropes that seemingly served different purposes—one to advocate against slavery and for Cuba's independence, and the other to support US intervention in Cuba—still used similar discursive patterns at the cusp of an emergent US empire. In the context of transamericanity, that these seemingly opposing narratives reify similarly emplotted narratives about Cuba points to the discursive power of these gothicized discourses at that time.

---

51. Lazo, *Writing to Cuba*, 191.
52. Wilcox, "Cuba's 'Hot Little Rebel,'" 156.

CHAPTER FIVE

"Inside the Monster"

José Martí's Decolonial Transamericanity

LITTLE MORE than a year after José Martí wrote his famous 1894 essay "La verdad sobre los Estados Unidos" [The Truth about the United States], based on his nearly fifteen years in exile, he made his way back to Cuba. After living mostly in New York City as a correspondent for many Latin American newspapers, and against all caution to the contrary, Martí insisted on joining the fray in the armed struggle for the island's independence from Spain, which had erupted again in early 1895. His most famous and oft-quoted representation of the United States is found in his last letter, of May 18, 1895, written to a friend in Mexico the day before he was killed in a firefight with Spanish soldiers in Dos Ríos, Cuba. In that unfinished letter, Martí wrote:

> Ya estoy todos los días en peligro de dar mi vida por mi país y por mi deber [. . .] de impedir a tiempo con la independencia de Cuba que se extiendan por las Antillas los Estados Unidos y caigan, con esa fuerza más, sobre nuestras tierras de América. Cuanto hice hasta hoy, y haré, es para eso. (1)

> Every day now I am in danger of giving my life for my country and my duty [. . .] in order to prevent, by the timely independence of

Cuba, the United States from extending its hold across the Antilles and falling with all the greater force on the lands of our America. All I have done up to now and all I will do is for that. (347)

In dramatic language, Martí cast himself as a martyr in the anti-imperialist cause and presciently noted that he was fighting on two fronts. The struggle, he said, was against Spain's centuries-old colonial oppression of Cuba, and also against the possibility of a US takeover of an independent Cuba as its portal into the Caribbean. In that way, Martí articulated a transcolonial range of view, one that trained its sights not only on Spanish colonialism but also on the greater challenge of a US imperialist expansion into the Americas.

As a response to growing anxieties at century's end about US intervention in the hemisphere, which Martí had articulated earlier in two of his most famous and prophetic essays, he represented the fledgling empire in gothicized terms. In that final letter to his friend Manuel Mercado, he wrote:

> Los pueblos—como ese de Vd. y mío,—más vitalmente interesados en impedir que en Cuba se abra, por la anexión de los Imperialistas de allá y los españoles, el camino que se ha de cegar, y con nuestra sangre estamos cegando, de la anexión de los pueblos de nuestra América, al Norte revuelto y brutal que los desprecia [. . .]. Viví en el monstruo, y le conozco las entrañas:—y mi honda es la de David. (1)

> The nations such as your own and mine, —have the most vital interest in keeping Cuba from becoming, through an annexation accomplished by those imperialists and the Spaniards, the doorway—which must be blocked and which, with our blood, we are blocking—to the annexation of the peoples of our America by the turbulent and brutal North that holds them in contempt. I lived in the monster, and I know its entrails—and my sling is the sling of David. (347)

Utilizing the trope of monstrosity to represent the United States, Martí equates himself to a biblical hero who prevailed over impossible odds, sharply dichotomizing the hemispheric conflict in terms of good and evil. Martí feared that, freed from one colonial master, Cuba would fall prey to a stronger, more "brutal" predator lurking in the hemisphere, one the island would not be able to defeat. Regionalizing the United States as a dangerous "North" in opposition to Latin America and the Caribbean, Martí gothicized the US nation as a monstrous cultural and political adversary poised to violently subjugate the hemisphere.

In this chapter, I examine how Martí used tropes of fear—especially the figure of the monster—to represent the looming political and cultural danger of the United States to the hemisphere. I specifically focus on how Martí deployed the language of fear to turn the rhetorical tables at a time when a gothicized Cuba had been transformed discursively from a potentially dangerous influence on the United States into a vulnerable victim of Spain. By deploying similar discursive strategies—that is, by utilizing tropes of dangerousness, monstrosity, and imperiled women, but doing so to negatively represent the United States—Martí was a key contributor to the figurative simultaneities this study has focused on within nineteenth-century transamericanity. In addition, not only was Martí's perspective actively transcolonial—simultaneously in opposition to Spanish and US imperialisms—but he also engaged in what I call a *decolonial transamericanity*. To that end, Martí represented the "neighbor to the North" as more dangerous and monstrous than anything that could be imagined in relation to Cuba or Latin America. Martí, like other writers in this study who figured the island as a damsel in distress, also drew from fear-based representations that imbricated race, gender, and nation (or, in his case, the hemisphere) to signal Otherness, but he did so to advocate for a unifying factor that would enable them to contest US actions and influence.

In arguing for the difference between a hemispheric America and the United States, Martí sought to decolonize the discourses of transamericanity, and he supported his argument through three main concepts:

- First, he made ontological claims of identity—similar to those used by other writers in this study to represent Cuba as dangerous—that imbricated race, gender, and hemispheric identity set in opposition to a dangerous "North," which also was represented as corruptive.

- In the fight against US imperialism in the region, he argued for contextualizing the local within the global as he envisioned the political, cultural, and ideological anticolonial unification of the Americas.
- Finally, and similar to other writers in this study, Martí used gothicized and other fear-based imagery at the same time that he gendered the hemisphere as a woman in peril and the United States as a male aggressor.

In these ways, and at the heart of his rhetorical strategy, Martí used well-known tropes of fear but inverted their usual targets to construct a discursive structure that would inspire Cubans and Latin Americans to resist US colonialist incursion in the region.

In developing the notion of Martí's decolonial transamericanity, I draw from Aníbal Quijano's concept of "decoloniality," or how knowledge must be decolonized to counter "the coloniality of world power," primarily through an "epistemological decolonization" that involves recognizing how "master paradigms are just but options dressed with universal clothes."[1] By challenging the universalization of "master" narratives, such as the naturalized oppositions between good/bad, civilized/savage, and colonizer/colonized, the "decolonial option," as Walter Mignolo has described it, promotes "a different type of thinking" that actively employs "epistemic disobedience," that is, a rejection of the naturalized subservience to dominant epistemologies.[2] In my reading, by taking the colonizer's own ideological rationales and using them to counter not just colonialism but also the discourses of coloniality within transamericanity, Martí exemplifies an epistemological "disobedience" that is hemispherically decolonial.

Martí's discursive reversion principally reclaims the figure of the monster, which had long been associated with Eurocentric constructs of the "New World," or the Americas. Persephone Braham persuasively observes how "whole regions of Latin America—Amazonia, Patagonia, the Caribbean—are named for monsters: women warriors, big-footed giants, and consumers of human flesh."[3] Further, Braham argues that while monsters are "found in virtually all of the world's sacred tradi-

---

1. Quijano, "Coloniality and Modernity/Rationality," 31.
2. Mignolo, "Introduction: Coloniality of Power and De-Colonial Thinking," 2.
3. Braham, "Making Monsters," 1.

tions, [. . .] only in Latin America did Amazons, cannibals, zombies, and other monsters become enduring symbols of national and regional characters." Within the colonial contact zone, monsters embodied "exoticism, hybridity, and sexual and other excesses," conceptualizing "the unknown" in ways that paved the way for conquest.[4] The etymology of "the word—from the Latin "*monstrar[e]* (to demonstrate), *monere* (to admonish), and *monstrum* (a warning or portent)"—points to how monsters become cultural "signposts that alert us to hidden truths."[5] In keeping with the monster's nature to demonstrate, admonish, and warn, Martí drew on this ideologically vested figure to represent neither Cuba nor Latin America, as was commonplace within transamericanity, but the United States, in ways that signposted its "hidden truths" to issue a hemispheric call for anti-imperialist action.

Here, I focus primarily on his most famous 1891 essay "Our America," in which Martí used the language of fear in relation to fairy tales to represent the "Northern neighbor" as a "seven-leagues giant" poised to stomp on the hemisphere. Then I examine his 1894 essay "The Truth about the United States," in which Martí conjured the idea of "monster" nations that would imitate the United States and thereby imperil their own cultural and national identities. I conclude with Martí's final letter, with which I introduced this chapter, and which contains his most quoted figuration of the United States as a "monster" within whose "entrails" he had lived. As we see throughout these texts, his figuration of the "neighbor to the North" became more gothicized as his concern over the imminent rise of a US empire in the region became more urgent.

Born in 1853 to a poor Spanish military officer and his Canary Islands-born wife, Martí received an education because his godfather paid for him to study at a Havana school. After writing a letter that accused a fellow student of being pro-Spanish, Martí was arrested and jailed. In 1870, he was tried by a military court and sentenced to six years of hard labor, but was pardoned after one year for health reasons. Spanish officials deported the teenaged Martí in 1871 to Spain, where he obtained a law degree and a doctorate in Philosophy and Humanities. Because he was banned from returning to his native Cuba, Martí traveled to Mexico, where he worked as a journalist and where

---

4. Braham, "Making Monsters," 1, 2.
5. Braham, "Making Monsters," 2.

he first began to gain a regional reputation as a writer and thinker.[6] By 1879, Martí was referring to Cuba as "Our Nation," and advocating for independence rather than for autonomy, which got him arrested and deported again to Spain, where he was imprisoned. After escaping from prison, Martí traveled to Paris, and then to the United States, where he settled in New York City for the last fourteen years of his life. In New York, he became a correspondent for several Latin American newspapers, and also wrote for *the New York Sun*. Philip S. Foner, one of Martí's anthologists and biographers, notes that Martí's work is unique because no other writer "had previously had such a chance to interpret the United States to so many people in Latin America, and through [newspapers] published in the United States, to Latin Americans in this country."[7] Martí's transamerican reach makes his gothicized representations of the United States significant to this study. This is especially so because Martí's perspective was shaped as much by his direct experience with Spanish political repression as by his living and working in the United States.[8]

Within that frame of reference, Martí's vision was decidedly transcolonial in that it transcended the borders of any one colonialist or imperialist hegemony. Sarah E. Johnson has noted the connection between "transcoloniality" and the "communication networks that flourished in the interstices of empires, calling into question strict colonial loyalties or imperialist isolation."[9] Further, Johnson defines "transcoloniality as both a geopolitical and a methodological concept," one that "describes the conflicts and collaborations that occurred between the residents of American territories governed by separate political entities."[10] As a methodology, Johnson suggests that transcoloniality "provides a counternarrative to the linguistically and disciplinarily isolated fields of American and Caribbean studies that still tend to compartmentalize the region according to [colonially based]

---

6. Foner, *Inside*, 21 24.
7. Foner, *Inside*, 27, 29, 30.
8. Spangler and Schwarzmann show the unparalleled breadth and scope of Martí's journalistic production during his nearly fifteen years in New York, noting that he "sent over 200 articles on life in the United States to a variety of international newspapers," at the same time that he wrote for Spanish-language newspapers within the United States. Spangler and Schwarzmann, *Syncing the Americas*, 3.
9. Johnson, *The Fear of French Negroes*, 1.
10. Johnson, *The Fear of French Negroes*, 2–3.

categories."¹¹ In earlier work, Francois Lionnet defined the transcolonial as a lens that focuses on "the spatial dimensions at the heart of the history of colonialism," at the same time that it privileges "a relational approach that takes the form of networks among sites marked differentially by the imperial project and the colonial will to power."¹² I use the term transcolonial to identify Martí's immersion in a particular geopolitical moment of competing and interconnected empires, as well as to categorize the methods he used to analyze the operations of imperial power across different colonial contexts. Martí's transcolonial writings articulate a decidedly decolonial approach, one that rejected all colonialisms (and colonialities) as he advocated for Cuba's sovereignty and for the freedom of the entire Americas from any and all political or cultural shackles.

But before Martí acquired the transcolonial perspective that represented the United States as a threat to the entire hemisphere, and like the *filibustero* novelist Cirilo Villaverde before him, Foner points out how he was initially "attracted, even dazzled" by US democracy, as well as "its creative power, and the opportunity it provided for every kind of individual initiative.¹³ In 1880, upon first arriving in the United States, Martí wrote: "At last I am here in a country where everyone seems to be his own master." However, Martí's first-hand experiences with and his observations of US life soon eroded that initial admiration. Eventually, he realized that his original concept of the United States, which was shared by many others in Latin America, "was in need of revision."¹⁴ Having reached this conclusion, Martí set himself to the project of correcting the way in which the United States was perceived by its hemispheric neighbors.

In addition to being a keen political observer, Martí was also a vocal admirer, avid reader, critic, and translator of US literature, which provided another source of information and perspective. Martí wrote literary portraits of renowned US authors, such as Ralph Waldo Emerson, Walt Whitman, Henry Wadsworth Longfellow, and Louisa May Alcott, although the last of these was never published. Working for Appleton & Co., Martí translated poems by Emerson, Whitman, and Edgar Allan

---

11. Johnson, *The Fear of French Negroes*, 3.
12. Lionnet, "Narrating," 69.
13. Foner, *Inside*, 31.
14. Foner, *Inside*, 32.

Poe into Spanish; translated portions of Emerson's essays and Alcott's *Hospital Sketches*; and translated Helen Hunt Jackson's novel *Ramona*, among other contemporary works.[15] In his job as US correspondent for about twenty newspapers across Latin America, Martí made it his mission to "define, notify, caution, [and] reveal the secrets of this country's successes, which are marvelous in appearance, and in appearance only."[16] Oscar Montero has argued that central to Martí's writings is the "tension between arts and politics," which is also central to many of the works examined in this study.[17] Politics was at the heart of Martí's representations of the United States, as he wanted to show his readers that admiration for the northern neighbor was based on a superficial understanding. This created a tension in Martí between his deep admiration for US literature and his rejection of many aspects of US culture and politics.[18]

In rejecting US influence in the region, Martí identified an ontological difference between Latin America and the United States, which is at the core of his most famous essay, "Our America." Martí begins by drawing on the tropes of fear associated with fairy tales, similar to how Julian Hawthorne framed Evangelina Cisneros's narrative in the previous chapter. In doing so, Martí personifies the Latin American nations as "the prideful villager," who "thinks his hometown contains the whole world." He juxtaposes the villager's too-narrow view to "the giants in seven-league boots who can crush him underfoot" (288). Here, Martí appears to draw from the "Tom Thumb" fairy tale, in which the tiny child steals an ogre's "seven-league boots" to defeat the giant. But unlike the cunning Tom Thumb in the fairy tale, the Latin American villager is powerless and in mortal danger from Martí's imagined giant. Along similar lines, Martí builds on fantastical imagery, noting that this villager also is oblivious to "the battling comets in the heavens that go through the air devouring the sleeping worlds" (288). The "giants"

---

15. Fountain, *José Martí and U.S. Writers*, 23, 25.
16. Kirk, "José Martí and the United States," 283.
17. Montero, *José Martí*, 3.
18. Spangler and Schwarzmann argue that Martí wrote about US writers and books for Latin American newspapers in an effort "to sync the two Americas intellectually and create cultural commonality" as a way "to disseminate modern ideas in Latin America and to reawaken and spur its cultural energies, which had been subjugated by centuries of colonial rule." Spangler and Schwarzmann, *Syncing the Americas*, ix.

and "the battling comets" serve as metaphors for competing imperialist nations which, Martí noted, would not only "crush" smaller nations, but also "devour" those that failed to notice this conflict. This image, Montero argues, is Martí's way of critiquing Latin Americans for being "ignorant of a universal order," and of warning them that such ignorance imperiled them.[19] For Montero, Martí's "transcendental vision" in this essay separates it "from the crowded archive of anti-imperialist tracts" of the time.[20] Martí's work is also transcendental, I would add, because he drew from well-known tropes of fear to craft a decolonial transamericanity that directly engaged with and challenged geopolitical discourses of the time.

By establishing this binary between the "sleepy hometown in America," and the destructive imperialist forces represented through the language of legend and science fiction, Martí fused the local to the global (*Selected Writings,* 288). He cautioned that the limited perspective of the village or hometown was insufficient for the geopolitical context of contending imperialisms in the late nineteenth century. He advocated for a broader transamerican—and transcolonial—perspective as necessary for both national *and* hemispheric survival. To achieve this, Martí argued for decolonizing knowledge through the use of intellectual "weapons of the mind, which vanquish all others" (288). Jeffrey Belnap and Raúl Fernández observe that Martí's "overlapping identities as a revolutionary activist and as a transnational journalist taught him to see the struggle for Cuban independence as part of an elaborate geopolitical puzzle," in which what was originally seen as "national" had to be recast "as a local inflection of a transnational phenomenon that can be read according to a hemispheric dialectic."[21] The transamerican context in which Martí wrote, and the transcolonial perspective he promoted, enabled him to incorporate the local into the global as part of his decolonial approach.

Also against this backdrop, Martí envisioned a hemispheric alliance in which the Latin American "hometowns," which distrusted and hated one another, had to "become acquainted, like men who are about to do battle" (288). Utilizing the notion of brothers in arms that fight a common enemy, Martí added: "Those who shake their fists at each other

---

19. Montero, *José Martí,* 94.
20. Montero, *José Martí,* 94.
21. Belnap and Fernández, *José Martí,* 4.

like jealous brothers quarreling over a piece of land [. . .] must join hands and interlace them until their two hands become one" (288). Martí's perspective, as Susana Rotker argues, "generally ignores the marked differences among Spanish American nations and politics" so that he can re-envision the hemisphere "as a cohesive unit." Rotker posits that through this erasure of differences in Spanish America, Martí developed the political concept of a formidable nation-of-nations, his idea of "Our America," based on an "us-and-them" binary where the "us" functioned as a "site of power" to challenge the colonizing "them," and which refused the category of "I-as-the-Other." By representing the United States as an "Other" to Latin America, Martí positioned himself as the writer who could gaze critically at imperial power because he lived *within* the empire. This rhetorical stance is characteristic of the decolonial strategies Martí employed in his writing to shatter traditional expectations of what the binaries of "powerful/powerless, center/periphery," and colonizer/colonized represented.[22] Further, Martí presented his positionality as an exiled Latin American as an asset because by being in the midst of the imperialist "them," he gained the information and perspective necessary to advance a decolonial option.

The ontological differences Martí established among US, European, and Latin American identities were based on the epistemological opposition between the natural (which he identified with Latin America) and the unnatural (which he related to colonial powers). Martí argued that forms of government "must be in harmony with the country's natural constitution" because "government is no more than an equilibrium among the country's natural elements." For Martí, these "natural" elements were self-evident in Latin America, and in opposition to what he called "the imported book." Thus, he added: "The battle is not between civilization and barbarity, but between false erudition and nature." Rejecting the civilized/barbarous opposition proposed in 1845 by the Argentine Domingo F. Sarmiento in *Facundo: Or, Civilization and Barbarism*, Martí countered that the important clash was between nature and nurture.[23] Further, he argued that nature is more

---

22. Rotker, *The American Chronicles of José Martí*, 84, 85, 86, 87, 102.

23. Sarmiento's *Facundo: Or, Civilization and Barbarism*, first published in 1845 as a biography of the *gaucho* Juan Facundo Quiroga, was translated in 1868 by Mary Peabody Mann, the author of *Juanita*, whose novel I examine in chapter 3. In his

significant because it reveals an ontology that cannot and should not be altered by a corruptively colonizing nurture.

This colonialist dependence on "the imported book," Martí feared, provided the wrong type of nurture to the Latin American nature, resulting in ineffectual and even self-destructive behavior. His main concern was that American "youth go out into the world wearing Yankee- or French-colored glasses and aspire to rule by guesswork a country they do not know." The real need of all Latin American countries, Martí noted, was to know their own history "from the Incas to the present [. . .] in its smallest detail, even if the Greek Archons [rulers of Athens] go untaught" (291). The hemispheric "American university" Martí envisioned was one where Western history and culture would no longer hold a privileged position. Instead, Latin American youth would be educated in the history and politics of their own countries from their indigenous beginnings to the present time. This epistemic re-envisioning, Martí believed, would redress the "grave blunders" that have led "the colony" to live on "in the republic," as he described the infectious neocolonial experience while prescribing its decolonial antidote.

America, Martí suggested, would not become truly decolonized until it ceased to look toward empires for its political and cultural models. This "excessive importation of foreign ideas and formulas" meant that in Spanish America "the republic [still] struggles against the colony" (293). Anticipating twentieth-century postcolonial theorists and the concept of neocolonialism, Martí argued that despite its postcolonial status, Latin America would never rid itself of its colonized mentality until it refashioned itself on its own terms.[24] Martí

---

introduction to the 2002 edition of Sarmiento's work, Stavans notes: "For Sarmiento, the consummate Europeanized Latin American intellectual, these two words described a land [Argentina] torn by a divided loyalty: the desire to emulate Europe and the urge to pursue the unruly, chaotic behavior symbolized by the primitivism of the Americas." Stavans, "Introduction," xiv. Goodrich notes how Sarmiento met Peabody Mann in 1847, and in 1865, shortly after his arrival in the United States as Argentinian ambassador, asked her to translate his text into English. Over the forty-year expanse of their friendship, Peabody Mann and Sarmiento exchanged nearly four hundred letters. This experience in transamerican translation gave Mary the discursive tools she used in *Juanita* to argue that Cuba was an inherently "barbaric" country, which could not be civilized by the United States. Goodrich, "From Barbarism to Civilization."

24. See Fanon, *Black Skins, White Masks* and Thiong'o, *Decolonising the Mind*.

argued: "No Yankee or European book could furnish the key to the Hispanoamerican enigma" (294). In posing the Latin American ontology as an unresolved question, Martí invited his readers to prioritize the development of decolonizing answers. For him, Latin American self-knowledge would be achieved not through existing colonialist figurations but through the epistemic challenge of delving into the particularities of what he saw as their specific "nature."

In representing "Our America" through this structure of dichotomized ontologies, and in using it to express his anxieties regarding the hemisphere's internal/internalized coloniality, Martí gendered the Americas as an imperiled woman when discussing the external dangers to the region from a rising US empire. Martí wrote:

> Pero otro peligro corre, acaso, nuestra América, que no le viene de sí, sino de la diferencia de orígenes, métodos e intereses entre los dos factores continentales, y es la hora próxima en que se le acerque, demandando relaciones íntimas, un pueblo emprendedor y pujante que la desconoce y la desdeña. (32)

> But our America may also face another danger, which comes not from within but from the differing origins, methods, and interests of the continent's two factions. The hour is near when she will be approached by an enterprising and forceful nation that will demand intimate relations with her, though it does not know her and disdains her. (294–95)

Using tropes of fear that—like other writers in this study who gothicized Cuba as a damsel in distress—call to mind the threat of sexual assault, Martí gendered the hemisphere as feminine to metaphorically represent the impending clash between the "two factions": one masculinized as dangerous and the other feminized as imperiled. By gendering the Americas in this way, Martí invoked the fear of a woman's represented inability to resist a more physically powerful foe bent on sexually possessing her.

The impending sexual violence that he suggests here contrasts with his earlier gendering of the "natural man" as the one responsible for securing the future of the Americas on his own terms. While Martí invests the natural man with agency to effect and represent change,

America-as-woman depends on seeking the support of others to save herself. For Martí, the "virile nations self-made by the rifle and the law love other virile nations, and love only them" (295). This queered image of "virile" nations loving only those who are similarly strong was counterpoised against the fear of America-as-woman being "despised" by the United States because of its perceived weakness. Martí builds on that sexual imagery, noting:

> Como la hora del desenfreno y la ambición, de que acaso se libre, por el predominio de lo más puro de su sangre, la América del Norte, o en que pudieran lanzarla sus masas vengativas y sórdidas, la tradición de conquista y el interés de un caudillo hábil, no está tan cercana aún a los ojos del más espantadizo, que no dé tiempo a la prueba de altivez, continua y discreta, con que se la pudiera encarar y desviarla. (32)

> The hour of unbridled passion and ambition from which North America may escape by the ascendency of the purest elements in its blood [. . .] is not yet so close, even to the most apprehensive eye, that there is no time for it to be confronted and averted by the manifestation of a discrete and unswerving pride (295)

This imagined sexual assault on the feminized Americas, Martí suggests, is checked only because of US concern about its global reputation, and depends solely on the demureness of America-as-woman. Like other writers in this study, who imbricated race, gender, and nation to raise fears about Cuba's influence, Martí draws on gendered tropes of fear to elicit anxiety about America's peril because of the United States. However, Martí deployed this language of fear differently: not just to represent the Americas as weaker and imperiled but also to persuade Latin Americans to take a strong, united stance against US imperialism.

Further illuminating the centrality of his imbrications of race, gender, and nationality to this fear-based argument, Martí added that to avoid being taken by force, America's "urgent duty" was "to show herself as she is, one in soul and intent, rapidly overcoming the crushing weight of her past, and stained only by the fertile blood shed by hands that do battle against ruins" (295). America-as-woman, in Martí's imagination, had to be pure and unstained, except for bloodying herself in the act of rebuilding from her past. However, although Martí identified the United States as the aggressor, and stereotyped America using the gendered trope of threatened victim, he did not ultimately cast the Americas in that role. In Martí's telling, America is allowed to be the heroine of her own story and has a clear obligation: to make the male-gendered United States respect her so that he will not perceive her as a sexual object. Martí suggests that only by showing how she has overcome her colonial past can America-as-woman argue for her equal place next to what he had described as the "seven-league-boots giant."

In "Our America," Martí builds on the language of fear in fairy tales to represent both men (the villagers) and women (the hemisphere) as endangered by their own unexamined behavior, advocating self-knowledge and self-advocacy against the corruptive influences of coloniality. In training his transcolonial gaze "bifocally," both inwards to Latin America and outwards to the United States, Martí employed the language of fear and reversed the ways in which it had been utilized within transamericanity. The essay further shows how Martí's transcoloniality had a stereophonic quality (to draw from Paul Gilroy's concept of "the black Atlantic"), enabled by the fact that he was fighting imperialism on two major fronts.[25] In "Our America," Martí's transcolonial vision, one that recognized the neocolonial effects of coloniality in its psychological and political legacies, is enabled by the bifocal context in which he lived and wrote.

In returning to the idea of US corruptive influence and danger in his 1894 essay "The Truth about the United States," Martí drew more fully on the gothicized trope of monstrosity. Fearing that "an excessive love for the North," resulting from "the imprudent and understandable expression of a desire for progress," would lead Latin American nations to adopt concepts that did not fit their reality, Martí added "that ideas, like trees, must grow from deep roots, and must be adapted to the soil in which they are planted in order to grow and prosper" (331). Not-

---

25. See Gilroy, *The Black Atlantic*, 3. Gilroy describes the heuristic of "the black Atlantic world" as one that addresses "the stereophonic, bilingual, or bifocal cultural forms originated by, but no longer the exclusive property of, [dispersed] blacks," and which records "the special stress that grows with the effort involved in trying to face (at least) two ways at once" (3). Martí's writings decidedly show the bifocality that Gilroy underscores.

ing that "the newborn is not fed the strong spices of adulthood only because the mustache and sideburns of adulthood are playfully hung on his soft face," Martí observed that only "monsters are created thus, not nations: we must live our own lives and sweat out our own fevers" (331). The idea of "sweating out" their own disease, rather than applying US models to redress their problems, articulates Martí's notion that, to avoid becoming monstrous, Latin American nations had to learn from their own mistakes rather than pretending to be someone else, like a child playing dress up. For Martí, the failure to acknowledge and value their hemispheric experience in favor of unquestioningly adopting US mores and ideas would have corruptive and deformative effects on Latin Americans. In this way, Martí issued an epistemic salvo against the naturalized notion that the United States was a heroic model of freedom and progress.

In utilizing the gothicized image of the monster, Martí argued that it was "urgent that our America learn the truth" about its northern neighbor. Drawing on what he had already signified in "Our America" as the binary opposition between Latin America and the United States, Martí further racialized the conflict in terms of "Latins" and "Saxons." However, he complicated this racialization by claiming that both "have an equal capacity for virtues and defects" (329). Montero has observed how, while Martí argued against a biological conception of race, when it came to signifying the differences between the United States and Latin America, he drew on racial and cultural distinctions. For Montero, this was a tactical strategy, inspired by Martí's knowledge of how central the concept of race was in the United States's self-conception, and because he knew of "the persistence of race-hatred in the politics and culture of the United States." Because "he knew that prejudices based on racial and cultural differences figured prominently in discussions about the role of the United States in Latin America," Montero believes that Martí used race as a signifier to argue for racial equality, but also simultaneously to represent the cultural differences between the two regions as unbridgeable.[26]

In crafting a decolonial counter-representation of Latin America to challenge its figuration as racially inferior to the United States, Martí juxtaposes the region to the US South. Specifically, Martí wrote:

---

26. Montero, *José Martí*, 103, 104.

> En lo que se ha de ver si sajones y latinos son distintos, y en lo que únicamente se les puede comparar, es en aquello en que se les hayan rodeado condiciones comunes: y es un hecho que en los Estados del Sur de la Unión Americana, donde hubo esclavos negros, el carácter dominante es tan soberbio, tan perezoso, tan inclemente, tan desvalido, como pudiera ser, en consecuencia de la esclavitud, el de los hijos de Cuba. (2)

> The only way to find out whether Saxons and Latins are different, or to compare them, is by seeing how they have reacted under comparable conditions; and it is a fact that in the Southern states of the American Union, where there were black slaves, the predominant character of the people is as haughty, as idle, as tempestuous, and as helpless as the character of the sons of Cuba may be, as a result of slavery. (330)

In linking Cuba to the US South through the geoculture of slavery, Martí argued that US Americans and Latin Americans were equally infected by the history and culture of slavery and were, therefore, not very different from each other. Thereby, Martí sought to rebut the notion that only Cubans (or Latin Americans as a whole) were tainted by the geoculture of slavery, and countered US representations of Cuba as inferior and incapable of self-government because of its slave-based economy.

In addition, even as he represented Latin America as a unified whole, erasing national and cultural differences among its inhabitants, Martí argued that there was no such thing as "the United States." Martí wrote:

> Es de supina ignorancia, y de ligereza infantil y punible, hablar de los Estados Unidos, y de las conquistas reales o aparentes de una comarca suya o grupo de ellas, como de una nación total e igual, de libertad unánime y de conquistas definitivas: semejantes Estados Unidos son una ilusión, o una superchería. (2)

> It is a mark of supine ignorance and childish, punishable light-mindedness to speak of the United States, and of the real or apparent achievements of one of its regions or a group of them, as a total or

equal nation of unanimous liberty and definitive achievement; such a United States is an illusion or a fraud. (330)

Calling to mind the ways in which Latin America was represented in the United States as a divided, unequal, and subaltern region, Martí claimed that the idea of a unified and racially/culturally homogeneous United States was a concocted fiction. Worse, he added, it was a deception crafted with the intent to draw attention away from the historical, racial, and social forces that divided it as a nation. Martí supported this claim by drawing clear distinctions between the North and the South, noting that "there is a whole world between" them (330). By extension, he suggested that if there was a schism between North and South within the United States, then there could be no surprise in finding similar differences between North America and South America.

Notwithstanding this similarity, he differentiated the United States's experience from that of Latin America by noting how the former was an "unnatural federation," predicting that it would be transformed "into a harsh state of violent conquest" due to the "forced coexistence" of these oppositions, which only could result in "exacerbating and accentuating their primary differences" (330). In observing that "the bonds of union are loosening rather than tightening in the United States," Martí added that he was "not prophesying but attesting" (330). This assessment, decades after the US Civil War, did anticipate how the United States in 1898 would seek to coalesce and rally the nation through imperialist expansion abroad. In calling attention to these details, Martí sought to prevent "the American peoples of Spanish descent from falling, out of ignorance, bedazzlement, or impatience, [. . .] into an immoral, enfeebling servitude to a damaged and alien civilization," meaning the United States (331). Michael Hames-García has observed how Martí wanted "not only to demonstrate the difference between the United States and its southern neighbors for the purpose of proving that different peoples should take the paths appropriate to their own circumstances but also to disabuse others of myths and generalizations that he feels have grown up around the [United States]."[27] The truth, for Martí, was that the United States was not better than

---

27. Hames-García, "Which America," 21.

Latin America but actually worse, and therefore would be a corruptive and dangerous model for what the future of the Americas should be.

In his 1894 essay, Martí's purpose is to show that, in actuality, the same factors that were used to raise fears about Latin America (and Cuba)—such as the geoculture of slavery—were also at play in the United States, and he unveiled that correlation for the world to see. Further, Martí argued that the influence of the geoculture of slavery on the US character had caused it to devolve, using masculinist language to note that while "the North American character has declined since its independence, and is less humane and virile today, [. . .] the Hispanoamerican, from any point of view, is superior today" (332). Martí concludes by noting how his "Notes on the United States" would become "a permanent column" in the *Patria* newspaper so he could "demonstrate the two truths that are useful to our America: the crude, unequal, and decadent character of the United States, and the continual existence within it of all the violences, discords, immoralities, and disorders of which the Hispanoamerican peoples are accused" (333). Using this notion of the United States as a corruptive cultural force that would imperil Latin America, Martí turns the rhetorical tables and uses fear-based descriptions to represent it as a colonialist "monster."

In addition to representing the northern "neighbor" as a corruptive political and cultural force, Martí also used the trope of monstrosity to describe US urban life, in ways that promoted a type of urban gothic. In his analysis of Martí's writings in the United States, John Patrick Leary has discussed how the Cuban writer used the language of fear to portray "the ravenous beast of the subway, whose iron veins wind through the body of the city," thereby figuring "the grotesque commercialization of leisure," and signaling "aesthetic corruption."[28] Further, Leary has pointed to how Martí figured US city dwellers "in gothically monstrous terms," to show how "the poor are brutalized," and used the metaphor of "entrails" as his favorite way to signify "an intact self threatened by exploitation and mechanization." Leary also has observed how Martí portrayed "the downtown tenements, the piths of the Brooklyn Bridge (which he imagined as tombs for the 'unknown workers' [. . .] who died building the bridge), and the monstrous subway cars [as] the true 'insides' of the United States."[29] Like other writ-

---

28. Leary, *A Cultural History*, 82.
29. Leary, *A Cultural History*, 86.

ers in this study, Martí drew on tropes of fear, but, in his case, Martí moved away from gothicizing the natural world to emphasize the horrors of unfettered industrialism, thereby building on his ontological distinction between Latin America and the United States.

Finally, in the last letter, mentioned at the beginning of the chapter, Martí's depiction of himself as the biblical David signifies that, throughout the Americas, the anticolonial struggle against the United States was a God-given duty. By directly representing the larger nation as a "monster," Martí appears to compare himself to the biblical Jonah, who spent time inside a whale, noting how he had lived within the "entrails" of the empire. In discussing Martí's use of this gothicized language, Jesse Alemán has pointed out how "the presence of the other felt and discovered within rather than outside of the borders of self, home, and nation generates an inter-American gothic anxiety from 'inside the monster,' as Martí once described the United States."[30] By using this metaphor—of living in the viscera of the imperialist nation—Martí emphasizes his insider's knowledge and concomitantly his authority to persuasively warn against the United States. Living in the entrails of the monster, which allowed him to know what the gothicized creature needs to survive, invests Martí with the power of biblical heroes. Reversing the centuries-old discourses that associated Latin America with monstrosity, Martí personified the emergent empire as a destructive creature, as an enemy that had to be defeated before it could swallow them all.

This familiarity with the "entrails," the innermost and least appealing parts of a monstrous United States, enabled his bifocality and the decolonial transamericanity that he deployed in speaking against the powerful empire-on-the-rise. As a correspondent, Martí painted detailed and unflattering portraits of the United States through essays such as "The Lynching of the Italians," "A Town Sets a Black Man on Fire," "The Indians in the United States," and "Class War in Chicago: A Terrible Drama," among others. Describing Martí as a transamerican "cultural critic," José David Saldívar has observed the Cuban patriot's particular sensitivity "to the terrors and catastrophes of modernity wrought by slavery, the American Civil War, the US-Mexican War of 1846–48, and the conquests by the United States of the territories and

---

30. Alemán, "The Other Country" 2007, 78.

indigenous peoples of North America."[31] Indeed, Martí saw it as his purpose to educate his Latin American audience so it would come to know the United States as a complex, dangerous "neighbor," instead of only through its self-promoting rhetoric of progress, individual freedom, and republican government.

Because this study has focused on the use of fear-based and gothicized tropes within the geopolitical contest of a looming US empire in the Americas, my analysis here has centered on how Martí's literary tropes share and challenge similar representations within transamericanity. In that context, Martí's rhetorical choices contribute to our understanding of the simultaneities in the tropes of fear that arose and were used within the nineteenth-century transamerican imaginary. Moreover, within the context of a Global Latin/o Americas, Martí's gaze is foundational because he is among the first writers to use the term "Latins"—*los latinos, la gente Latina*—to underline the common links among Cubans, Puerto Ricans, Dominicans, Mexicans, and other Latin Americans who supported his efforts to liberate Cuba.[32] In conceptualizing these "Latins," Martí helped to give birth to a new identity—one that would bridge the schism he saw between Latin America and the United States—to represent the "continental soul" that he had dreamed of in "Our America" (296).

Indeed, as Laura Lomas has noted, Martí took on "the peculiar task of translating" the United States not only for "Spanish-language readers and audiences, but also for North Americans."[33] Within this context, Lomas uses the term "translation" to refer to Martí's "unavoidable, absolutely necessary shuttling between cultures," and to the "movements that transform the source and the target language texts," completely reshaping the way they are understood. Through his role as cultural translator, Martí became an early theorist in—even a principal interlocutor of—what we know today as the Latinx experience. This unique positionality enabled Martí to craft a decolonial transamericanity that, juxtaposed to the other texts in this study, provides an empowering articulation of the shared transamerican literary history of the time.

---

31. Saldívar, *Trans-Americanity*, 53.
32. Montero, *José Martí*, 10.
33. Lomas, *Translating Empire*, 29.

Within that literary history, the writers who gothicized Cuba, as I have shown, used tropes of fear to express anxieties about the geoculture of slavery within the context of a looming US empire. But while using similar signifiers, Martí envisioned Cuba and Latin America, united as a whole, not as victims but ultimately as powerful opponents to the dangerous and battling imperialist giants. Martí's rejection of the notions of US exceptionalism, Hames-García has argued, "should prompt us, as scholars of 'American literature,' to do the same."[34] For her part, Anne Fountain has called attention to how "John L. O'Sullivan's call in 1845 for the right [of the United States] to push west and south and impose Anglo dominance meets a defining response in José Martí," raising the question whether we should teach about Manifest Destiny without mentioning Martí.[35] Further, Fountain has observed that "the Cuba that formed José Martí's life was framed by Cuban desire for freedom from Spain, fear of US imperialism toward Cuba, and the continuing tragedy of slavery."[36] Added to Martí's life-changing experiences in the United States, these all fashioned him into the "transnational figure who continues to link the Americas."[37] As a contrapuntal juxtaposition to other texts in this study, Martí's re-vision of the United States introduces a foundational decolonial option to transamericanity, one that is as relevant and compelling today as it was two centuries ago.[38]

---

34. Hames-García, "Which America," 24.
35. Fountain, "José Martí, the United States," 117.
36. Fountain, "*José Martí and U.S. Writers*," 2.
37. Fountain, "*José Martí and U.S. Writers*," 20.
38. For Said, a "contrapuntal reading must take account of both processes, that of imperialism and that of resistance to it," and "each cultural work is a vision of a moment, and we must juxtapose that vision with the various revisions it later provoked." Said, *Culture and Imperialism*, 66–67.

CONCLUSION

Decolonizing the Gothic

IN A SHORT INTERVIEW for the *Kenyon Review* podcast series in November 2017, Junot Díaz discussed the significance of the gothic as a genre within the geocultural frame of a Global Latin/o Americas. In response to my question about the use of gothic tropes in his own writing, Díaz advocated for the importance of "young people to have a background and a grounding in the gothic, even more important in the postcolonial gothic, even more important in the decolonial gothic," noting the "ways in which our existence in the new world is so overdetermined by haunting, so overdetermined by specters, so overdetermined by those other elements of the gothic that are really important." For Díaz, the gothic does "a wonderful job explaining not only the stories that we've told about who we are as a nation but the stories that we tell about what we think history is." He notes the genre's usefulness in explaining his own experience "as a person of African descent, someone who looks back and there are more bodies, more dead, than there have ever been the living," someone who is "already always living a ghost story." In advocating for the significance of the gothic in a decolonial project, Díaz also articulates how the genre is inextricably linked to the geoculture of slavery in the Americas.[1]

---

1. Díaz, *Kenyon Review Podcast*. At the time of this interview, Díaz had not yet been publicly involved in the allegations of sexual misconduct and misogyny that

By introducing the idea of a gothic geoculture in relation to figurations of Cuba—that is, in the ways slavery and its aftermaths created a geocultural continuum across the hemisphere that was encoded through discursive simultaneities that relied on gothicized tropes—I have sought to identify a structure of meaning that opens further avenues of inquiry. Specifically, the idea of a gothic geoculture underlines the relevance of the geopolitical contexts of transamerican slavery and empire in understanding the concurrent representational equations—the corruptive gothicscapes, gothicized souths, transgressive hauntings, gothic emplotments, and decolonial approaches—developed by nineteenth-century writers throughout the hemisphere. And even while this project has focused mostly on gothicized figurations of Cuba that broke the mold of more traditional representations, the smaller scope does not argue against its significance. Indeed, while the rhetorical goals of many writers in this study were quite different, and while not all of them drew on the gothic in identical ways, all of the texts I examine crafted gothicized figurations that imbricated race, gender, and nationality, creating a mosaic of concurrencies within transamericanity. In considering these textual figurations of Cuba alongside more common and more extensively studied ones, we catalog the less recognized elements of transamericanity in the nineteenth century. This broader scope demonstrates a consistency in the ideologies of transamericanity that permeated throughout representations of Cuba, even as specific manifestations of those ideologies changed shape as the century unfolded and US imperial interests took new forms.

Also in that way, my project argues for conceiving of a more global gothic, one that encompasses the many subgenres—postcolonial, decolonial, transamerican, interamerican, imperial, regional, southern, Caribbean, hemispheric, US American, Latin American—increasingly engaged in dialogue with each other. As Díaz observed in his *Kenyon Review* interview, the gothic is uniquely situated not only to acknowledge and represent what transamericanity Othered, but also to unearth the ways in which that Othering has been connected to fear and horror and death.[2] In this paradigm, Atlantic slavery stands at the

---

surfaced in May 2018. See Phillips, "Pulitzer-Prize winning author." In a June story, Díaz denied all allegations. Shanahan and Ebbert, "Junot Díaz case may be a #MeToo turning point."

2. DeLaMotte has pointed out how "the rise and flowering of the Gothic novel in Britain and the U.S. between 1765 and 1850 coincides with the emergence and

very core as the engine that produced the geocultural contours of this study, because in creating Others for whom race, gender, and nationality were inherently fused, slavery in the Americas drew a sharp division between what was/is considered human/not-human.

Along those lines, in her recently published *The Origin of Others*, Toni Morrison pays particular attention to US slavery, observing how slave owners worked hard "to define the slave as inhuman, savage, when in fact the definition of the inhuman describes overwhelmingly the punisher" (29). Within this unavoidable duality, always already explained in racialized ways, she adds:

> The sensibility of the slave owners is gothic. It's as though they are shouting, "I am not a beast! I'm not a beast! I torture the helpless to prove I am not weak." The danger of sympathizing with the stranger is the possibility of becoming a stranger. To lose one's racial-ized rank is to lose one's own valued and enshrined difference. (30)

Slavery and its legacies, which this project has explored in literary and hemispheric terms, are integral to what Morrison describes as "the construction of the stranger and its benefits," and to how racialized discourses of Othering continue to wield discursive power, even today (19).[3]

In constructing the racialized Other, the figure of the monster has been instrumental, and especially connected to Latin America and the Caribbean, as I discussed in the previous chapter. Gabriel Eljaiek-Rodríguez notes how the gothic has employed "images and imaginaries that are related to the colonial and postcolonial relationship of Europe and the United States with Latin America (and vice versa), ideas that situate extreme otherness and monstrosity in the southern part of the continent."[4] More generally, and in addressing the historical grounding and "cultural shaping" of monsters, Leo Braudy posits that "each

---

codification of modern conceptions of 'race' as a biological division of humans into separate groups characterized by distinctive, non-overlapping physical, moral, intellectual, and emotional attributes." DeLaMotte, "White Terror, Black Dreams," 18.

3. In describing the "postcolonial gothic," Punter and Byron note: "The past, on [the gothic] view of history, is of course right in our midst; we see it in the form of contemporary debates around cultural and racial blame and apology." Punter and Byron, *The Gothic*, 56.

4. Eljaiek-Rodríguez, "Semillas de maldad," 14.

age has its own particular fears, and the history of horror is the history of the disquiets of the soul, the inner life, made public, taking on the colorations of the era in which they appear."[5] Further, he proposes that what is figured as monstrous and fearsome corresponds "to four prime areas of cultural anxiety in the Western world from the eighteenth century to the present": the "monster from nature," "the created monster," "the monster from within," and "the monster from the past." Monsters, he adds, are not isolated figures but "constitute a system of family resemblances that are modified according to the historical and cultural context in which they appear."[6] Within the context of nineteenth-century gothicized representations of Cuba, the transamerican imaginary drew from all four of these monstrosities. To craft a geocultural gothic, the represented monster was related to "nature" through landscape and geography, it was "created" by the geoculture of slavery, it was found "within" both interamerican and transamerican gothics, and it depended on "the past" as a primary though not the scariest site of haunting (since that belonged to a futurity at risk).

By focusing on writers who used gothicized figurations to represent Cuba, my project adds to a literary understanding of what John Patrick Leary has described as the "vexed" ways in which the "history and rhetoric of U.S. designs on Cuba, and Cuban creole interest in [and I would add, opposition to] annexation" were figured throughout the nineteenth century. In Leary's terms:

> The various ways in which Cuba is metaphorically domesticated, infantilized, Orientalized, and eroticized, in one instance praised as a splendorous, untouched Eden, and then denounced as a decadent, Catholic, Africanized barbarism, then celebrated as a modern, would-be republic groaning under Spanish tyranny, with its annexation to the United States rendered in the loftiest democratic rhetoric, show how dynamic were the cultural boundaries between Anglo-America and Spain's richest colony in the Americas. (37)

Leary eloquently catalogues the manifold and conflicting ways in which Cuba was signified within the context of US empire, and my project has argued for how the gothicized representations of the island are

---

5. Braudy, *Monsters*, 5.
6. Braudy, *Monsters*, 26.

squarely located within this particularly "vexed" context. In that way, the discursive creation of Cuba as a gothic geoculture responds directly to the geopolitical push and pull generated by the "battling comets" of José Martí's imagination, as mentioned in the previous chapter.[7]

In identifying the gothicized simultaneities within transamericanity, we find not only the "repeating island" that Antonio Benítez-Rojo has theorized, but also a repeating hemisphere, whose recursiveness is directly related—as Benítez-Rojo observed—to "the machine" of plantation slavery. In his own words, by proposing "a rereading of the Caribbean," Benítez-Rojo suggests

> partir del hecho de que las Antillas forman un puente de islas que conecta, de "cierta manera," Sudamérica con Norteamérica; es decir, una máquina de espuma que conecta las crónicas de la búsqueda de El Dorado con el relato del hallazgo de El Dorado; o también, si se quiere, el discurso del mito con el discurso de la historia, o bien, el discurso de la resistencia con el discurso del poder. (iii)

> as a point of departure the unargued fact that the Antilles are an island bridge connecting, 'in a certain way,' South and North America, that is, a machine of spume that links the narrative of the search for El Dorado with the narrative of the finding of El Dorado; or if you like, the discourse of myth with the discourse of history; or even, the discourse of resistance with the language of power. (4)

Being transamerican perforce implies exposure to what Gabriel García Márquez described as a "realidad descomunal" [outsized reality], the same that led many writers in this study to fuse fact with fiction to represent it.[8] It is at this hemispheric crossroads—between power and

---

7. Martí, like Villaverde, belongs to a tradition of Cuban literature in the United States that Cortina has noted "could easily be labelled Cuban exile literature," given that "there have been Cuban refugees living in the United States since the late eighteenth century." Cortina, "Cuban Literature of the United States," 69.

8. In his Nobel Prize Lecture in December 1982, García Márquez noted: "Poets and beggars, musicians and prophets, warriors and scoundrels, all creatures of that unbridled reality, we have had to ask but little of imagination, for our crucial problem has been a lack of conventional means to render our lives believable. This, my friends, is the crux of our solitude." See https://www.nobelprize.org/nobel_prizes/literature/laureates/1982/marquez-lecture.html.

resistance, myth and history, what is or is not categorized as gothic, and what is gothicized—that this project expands on the scholarly dialogue about how we read the many faces of transamericanity.

The larger-than-life geoculture produced by the colonial contact zone in the Americas conjures what Justin D. Edwards and Sandra Guardini Vasconcelos have described as the "double or multiple identities" throughout the hemisphere, which "underscore the linguistic and cultural variety that characterizes this vast territory." Further, they add, "The countries and nations comprehended within the idea of the 'tropics' share the common experience of having been forged from various European colonial and imperial projects."[9] Theorizing what they term as the "tropical gothic," Edwards and Guardini Vasconcelos argue that while "there is continuity between Gothic tropes from other regions and those found in the American tropics," the "tropical Gothic texts in the Americas have been mobilized in order to deal with the particular nature of the imperial and historical experience in this part of the world."[10] Similarly, while more expansively theorizing the "globalgothic" in a contemporary context, Glennis Byron has noted that while the genre "is obviously not unique in registering the effects of globalisation, it does appear to have a particularly intimate relationship with its processes, offering a ready-made language to describe whatever anxieties might arise in an increasingly globalised world."[11] Documenting the literary gothic geocultures that were produced by the globalizing forces of nineteenth-century slavery and empire offers another lens through which we can scrutinize the genre at a time when an increasing number of scholars are moving away from traditional US- and/or British-centered models to find broader and more far-reaching ways to understand the gothic.

In the end, by proposing that we recognize the geocultural gothic as a mode within the discourses of transamericanity, this study seeks to contribute a decolonial option, like the one Díaz advocates for. By identifying other, less studied ways in which the gothic was deployed in the Americas—particularly in relation to a location as overdetermined in representational terms as Cuba—this project sheds light on what Walter Mignolo has described as "the spaces that have been silenced,

---

9. Edwards and Guardini Vasconcelos, "Tropicalizing the Gothic," 3.
10. Edwards and Guardini Vasconcelos, "Tropicalizing the Gothic," 5.
11. Byron, *Globalgothic*, 2.

repressed, demonized, devaluated" by modern epistemologies.[12] Indeed, as Rodrigo Lazo and Jesse Alemán have argued, the "analytical framework" used to understand the Americas "should expand to encompass multiple traditions and nations, even multiple colonial legacies. Just as an Anglophone world has to contend with England, so does the explication of Hispanophone texts of the United States necessarily need to engage Spain and its colonial legacy."[13] In that vein, perhaps the most ambitious goal of this project is that, in shining a light into such gothicized spaces, we can learn more about how we—within the Global Latin/o Americas—have been Othered, have Othered ourselves, and have resisted/revised/rewritten such Otherings.

For the future, my hope is that as scholars and teachers of transamerican literature and of the discursive structures within transamericanity we lead the way by pursuing actively decolonial projects that, like Martí before us, counter and revise the monstrosity and Otherness too-long associated with the burden of embodying the failed utopia of a "New World." Upon the ashes of that imposed burden, I propose that we build the "opposite utopia" that García Márquez famously imagined through his uniquely powerful prose in his 1982 Nobel Prize Lecture:

> Una nueva y arrasadora utopía de la vida, donde nadie pueda decidir por otros hasta la forma de morir, donde de veras sea cierto el amor y sea posible la felicidad, y donde las estirpes condenadas a cien años de soledad tengan por fin y para siempre una segunda oportunidad sobre la tierra. (3)

> A new and sweeping utopia of life, where no one will be able to decide for others how they die, where love will prove true and happiness be possible, and where the races condemned to one hundred years of solitude will have, at last and forever, a second opportunity on earth. (3)

---

12. Mignolo and Escobar, *Globalization*, 2.
13. Lazo, "Historical Latinidades," 7.

BIBLIOGRAPHY

Ajuria Ibarra, Enrique. "Introduction: Exploring Gothic and/in Latin America." *Studies in Gothic Fiction* 3, no. 2 (2014): 6–10.

———. "Permanent hauntings: spectral fantasies and national trauma in Guillermo del Toro's *El espinazo del diablo* [The Devil's Backbone]." *Journal of Romance Studies* 12, no. 1 (2012): 56–71.

Alcott, Louisa May. *Louisa May Alcott: Her Life, Letters and Journals*. Edited by Ednah D. Cheney. Boston: Little, Brown, and Company, 1928.

——— and May Alcott. *Little Women Abroad: The Alcott Sisters' Letters from Europe, 1870–1871*. Edited by Daniel Shealy. Athens: The University of Georgia Press, 2008.

———. *Moods*. Edited by Sarah Elbert. New Brunswick: Rutgers University Press, 1999.

———. "Pauline's Passion and Punishment." In *Louisa May Alcott Unmasked: Collected Thrillers*, edited by Madeleine Stern. Boston: Northeastern University Press, 1995.

Aldana Reyes, Xavier. "Defining and Delimiting the Spanish Gothic." *Spanish Gothic: National Identity, Collaboration and Cultural Adaptation*. London: Palgrave Macmillan, 2017.

Alemán, Jesse. "The Other Country: Mexico, the United States, and the Gothic History of Conquest." *American Literary History* 18, no. 3 (2006): 406–26.

———. "The Other Country: Mexico, the United States, and the Gothic History of Conquest." In *Hemispheric American Studies*, edited by Caroline F. Levander and Robert S. Levine, 75–95. New Brunswick: Rutgers University Press, 2007.

——— and Shelley Streeby, eds. *Empire and the Literature of Sensation: An Anthology of Nineteenth-Century Popular Fiction.* New Brunswick: Rutgers University Press, 2007.

Alvarez-Amell, Diana. "Las dos caras de Cecilia Valdés: entre el romanticismo y el nacionalismo cubano." *Hispania* 83, no. 1 (2000): 1–10.

Anderson, Eric Gary, Taylor Hagood, and Daniel Cross Turner, eds. *Undead Souths: The Gothic and Beyond in Southern Literature and Culture.* Baton Rouge: Louisiana State University Press, 2015.

Ard, Patricia. Introduction. *Juanita: A Romance of Real Life in Cuba Fifty Years Ago,* by Mary Peabody Mann. 1887. Charlottesville: University of Virginia Press, 2000.

Badaracco, Claire M. Introduction. *The 'Cuba Journal' of Sophia Peabody Hawthorne,* Volume 1–3, edited from the manuscript with an introduction. Diss. Rutgers University, 1978.

———. "Sophia Peabody Hawthorne's Cuba Journal: Volume Three, 31 October 1834–15 March 1835." *Essex Institute: Historical Collections* 118 (1982): 280–318.

———. "'The Night-Blooming Cereus': A Letter from the 'Cuba Journal.'" *Bulletin of Research in the Humanities* 81, no. 1 (1978): 56–71.

Baker, Thomas N. *Sentiment & Celebrity: Nathaniel Parker Willis and the Trials of Literary Fame.* New York: Oxford University Press, 1998.

Ballou, Maturin N. *History of Cuba: or, Notes of a Traveller in the Tropics.* Phillips, Sampson & Co., 1854.

Bannett, Nina. "Cuban Femininity and National Unity in Louisa May Alcott's *Moods* and Elizabeth Stoddards's 'Eros and Anteros.'" In *Womanhood in Anglophone Literary Culture: Nineteenth and Twentieth Century Perspectives,* edited by Robin Hammerman. Newcastle upon Tyne: Cambridge Scholars, 2007.

Baptist, Edward E. *The Half Has Never Been Told: Slavery and the Making of American Capitalism.* Basic Books, 2014.

Beers, Henry A. *Nathaniel Parker Willis.* New York: Houghton Mifflin, 1885.

Beidler, Philip D. *The Island Called Paradise: Cuba in History, Literature, and the Arts.* Tuscaloosa: The University of Alabama Press, 2014.

Belnap, Jeffrey and Raúl Fernández. *José Martí's "Our America": From National to Hemispheric Cultural Studies.* Durham: Duke University Press, 1998.

Benítez-Rojo, Antonio. *La isla que se repite: El Caribe y la perspectiva postmoderna.* Ediciones del Norte, 1989.

———. *The Repeating Island: The Caribbean and the Postmodern Perspective.* Translated by James Maraniss. Durham: Duke University Press, 1996.

Berger, Tracy and Kathleen Guidroz, eds. *The Intersectional Approach: Transforming the Academy Through Race, Class, & Gender.* Chapel Hill: University of North Carolina Press, 2009.

Berzon, Judith R. *Neither White Nor Black: The Mulatto Character in American Fiction.* New York: New York University Press, 1978.

Biggio, Rebecca Skidmore. "The Specter of Conspiracy in Martin Delany's 'Blake.'" *African American Review* 42, nos. 3/4 (2008): 439–54.

Blanco, Maria del Pilar. *Ghost-Watching American Modernity: Haunting, Landscape, and the Hemispheric Imagination.* New York: Fordham University Press, 2012.

Blanco, Richard. "'Rum, Rumba, And Romance': A Book On Cuba's Enduring Mystique." *All Things Considered,* December 19, 2014, National Public Radio, https://www.npr.org/2014/12/19/371714205/a-book-on-cubas-enduring-mystique.

Braham, Penelope. "Making Monsters." *From Amazons to Zombies: Monsters in Latin America.* Lewisburg: Bucknell University Press, 2015.

Brantlinger, Patrick. *Rule of Darkness: British Literature and Imperialism, 1830–1914.* Ithaca: Cornell University Press, 1988.

Braudy, Leo. *Haunted: On Ghosts, Witches, Vampires, Zombies, and Other Monsters of the Natural and Supernatural Worlds.* New Haven: Yale University Press, 2016.

Bray, Katie. "'A Climate . . . More Prolific . . . in Sorcery': The Black Vampyre and the Hemispheric Gothic." *American Literature* 87, no. 1 (2015): 1–21.

Brickhouse, Anna. "'A Story of the Island of Cuba': William Cullen Bryant and the Hispanophone Americas." *Nineteenth-Century Literature* 56, no. 1 (2001): 1–22.

———. *Transamerican Literary Relations and the Nineteenth-Century Public Sphere.* Cambridge: Cambridge University Press, 2004.

Bryant, William Cullen. *Letters of a Traveller: or, Notes of Things Seen in Europe and America.* 1850. Filiquarian Publishing LLC, 2015.

———. "Story of the Island of Cuba." *The Complete Stories of William Cullen Bryant.* Hanover: University Press of New England, 2014.

Bryant, William Cullen II. *Power for Sanity: Selected Editorials of William Cullen Bryant, 1829–1861.* New York: Fordham University Press, 1994.

Buscaglia-Salgado, José F. *Undoing Empire: Race and Nation in the Mulatto Caribbean.* Minneapolis: University of Minnesota Press, 2003.

Byron, Glennis, ed. "Introduction." *Globalgothic.* Manchester, UK: Manchester University Press, 2013.

Cap, Piotr. *The Language of Fear: Communicating Threat in Public Discourse.* London: Palgrave Macmillan, 2017.

Casanova-Vizcaíno, Sandra and Inés Ortiz. "Latin America, the Caribbean, and the Persistence of the Gothic." *Latin American Gothic in Literature and Culture.* New York: Routledge, 2018.

Castillo, Susan and Charles L. Crow, eds. *The Palgrave Handbook of the Southern Gothic.* London: Palgrave Macmillan, 2016.

Castronovo, Russ, and Susan Gillman. *States of Emergency: The Object of American Studies.* Chapel Hill: University of North Carolina Press, 2014.

Chiles, Katy. "Within and Without Raced Nations: Intratextuality, Martin Delany, and 'Blake; Or, the Huts of America.'" *American Literature* 80, no. 2 (2008): 323–52.

Cisneros, Evangelina. *The Story of Evangelina Cisneros (Evangelina Betancourt Cosio y Cisneros, Told by Herself.* New York: Continental Publishing, 1897.

Cooper, Michaela B. "'Should Not These Things Be Known?': Mary Mann's Juanita and the Limits of Domesticity." In *Reinventing the Peabody Sisters,* edited by Monika M. Elbert, Julie E. Hall, and Katharine Rodier, 146–62. Iowa City: University of Iowa Press, 2006.

Cortina, Rodolfo J. "Cuban Literature of the United States 1824–1959." In *Recovering the US Hispanic Literary Heritage,* edited by Ramón Gutiérrez and Genaro Padilla, 69–88. Houston: Arte Público Press, 1993.

Council on Foreign Relations, *U.S.-Cuba Relations.* https://www.cfr.org/backgrounder/us-cuba-relations.

DeGuzmán, María. *Spain's Long Shadow: The Black Legend, Off-Whiteness, and Anglo-American Empire.* Minneapolis: University of Minnesota Press, 2005.

DeLamotte, Eugenia. "White Terror, Black Dreams: Gothic Constructions of Race in the Nineteenth Century." In *The Gothic Other: Racial and Social Constructions in the Literary Imagination,* edited by Ruth Bienstock Anolik and Douglas L. Howard, 17–31. Jefferson: McFarland & Co., 2004.

Delany, Martin R. *Blake, or the Huts of America,* edited by Floyd J. Miller. Boston: Beacon Press, 1970.

———. *Martin R. Delany: A Documentary Reader,* edited by Robert S. Levine. Chapel Hill: University of North Carolina Press, 2003.

Díaz, Junot. Interview by Ivonne M. García. *Kenyon Review Podcast.* October 9, 2017, https://www.kenyonreview.org/conversation/kr-podcast-with-junot-diaz.

Doolen, Andy. "'Be Cautious of the Word 'Rebel'": Race, Revolution, and Transnational History in Martin Delany's 'Blake; Or, the Huts of America.'" *American Literature* 81, no. 1 (2009): 153–79.

———. *Fugitive Empire: Locating Early American Imperialism.* Minneapolis: University of Minnesota Press, 2005.

Doyle, Christine. *Louisa May Alcott and Charlotte Brontë: Transatlantic Translations.* Knoxville: University of Tennessee Press, 2000.

Duncan, Cynthia. "The Fantastic as a Literary Genre." *Unraveling the Real: The Fantastic in Spanish-American Ficciones.* Philadelphia: Temple University Press, 2010.

Edwards, Justin D. *Gothic Passages: Racial Ambiguity and the American Gothic.* Iowa City: University of Iowa Press, 2003.

——— and Sandra Guardini Vasconcelos, eds. "Tropicalizing the Gothic." *Tropical Gothic in Literature and Culture: The Americas.* New York: Routledge, 2016.

Elbert, Monika and Bridget M. Marshall. *Transnational Gothic: Literary and Social Exchanges in the Long Nineteenth Century.* Farnham, UK: Ashgate, 2013.

Elbert, Sarah, ed. *Moods,* by Louisa May Alcott. New Brunswick: Rutgers University Press, 1999.

———. *Louisa May Alcott on Race, Sex, and Slavery.* Boston: Northeastern University Press, 1997.

Eljaiek-Rodríguez, Gabriel. "Semillas de maldad, Early Latin American Gothic." *Studies in Gothic Fiction* 3, no. 2 (2014): 13–23.

Ellis, Kate Ferguson. "Can You Forgive Her? The Gothic Heroine and Her Critics." In *A New Companion to the Gothic*, edited by David Punter, 455–68. New York: Blackwell Publishing, 2012.

Ellis, Markman. *The Politics of Sensibility: Race, Gender and Commerce in the Sentimental Novel.* Cambridge: Cambridge University Press, 1996.

Evans, J. Martin. *Milton's Imperial Epic: Paradise Lost and the Discourse of Colonialism.* Ithaca: Cornell University Press, 1996.

Fanon, Frantz. *Black Skins, White Masks.* 1952. New York: Grove Press, 1967.

Ferrer, Ada. *Insurgent Cuba: Race, Nation, and Revolution, 1868–1898.* Chapel Hill: University of North Carolina Press, 1999.

Fiedler, Leslie A. *Love and Death in the American Novel.* 1960. Champaign: Dalkey Archive Press, 2008.

Fischer, Sybille. "Introduction." Cirilo Villaverde. *Cecilia Valdés, or El Angel Hill: A Novel of Nineteenth-Century Cuba.* New York: Oxford University Press, 2005.

Forza, Daniela Ciani. "Sophia Peabody Hawthorne's 'Cuba Journal': A Link between Cultures." *Nathaniel Hawthorne Review* 37, no. 2 (2011): 73–96.

Fountain, Anne. *José Martí and U.S. Writers.* Gainesville: University Press of Florida, 2003.

———. *José Martí, the United States, and Race.* Gainesville: University Press of Florida, 2014.

Foxwell, Elizabeth. "Louisa May Alcott's Literary Double Life." *Mystery Scene* 54 (1996): 27–29.

García, Ivonne M. "Anticipating Colonialism: U.S. Letters on Puerto Rico and Cuba, 1831–1835." In *Letters and Cultural Transformations in the United States, 1760–1860,* edited by Theresa Strouth Gaul and Sharon M. Harris, 57–76. Farnham, UK: Ashgate Publishing, 2009.

———. "Gothic Cuba and the Trans-American South in Louisa May Alcott's 'M. L.'" In *The Palgrave Handbook of the Southern Gothic,* edited by Susan Castillo Street and Charles L. Crow, 161–74. London: Palgrave Macmillan, 2016.

———. "Transnational Crossings: Sophia Hawthorne's Authorial Persona from the 'Cuba Journal' to *Notes in England and Italy.*" *Nathaniel Hawthorne Review* 37, no. 2 (2011): 97–120.

———. "'With the Eyes That Are Given Me': Feminist Transcolonial Poetics in Sophia Peabody's The Cuba Journal." In *Toward a Female Genealogy of Transcendentalism,* edited by Jana L. Argersinger and Phyllis Cole, 59–78. Athens: The University of Georgia Press, 2014.

García Márquez, Gabriel. "La soledad de America Latina." *Nobel Lecture,* December 8, 1982, https://www.nobelprize.org/nobel_prizes/literature/laureates/1982/marquez-lecture.html.

———. "The Solitude of Latin America." *Nobel Lecture,* December 8, 1982, https://www.nobelprize.org/nobel_prizes/literature/laureates/1982/marquez-lecture.html.

Gelpí, Juan G. "El discurso jerárquico en *Cecilia Valdés.*" *Revista de Crítica Literaria Latinoamericana* 34 (1991): 47–61.

Gilroy, Paul. *The Black Atlantic: Modernity and Double Consciousness.* Cambridge: Harvard University Press, 1993.

Goddu, Teresa A. *Gothic America: Narrative, History, and Nation.* New York: Columbia University Press, 1997.

———. "Letters Turned to Gold: Hawthorne, Authorship, and Slavery." *Studies in American Fiction* 29, no. 1 (2001): 49–76.

Goodrich, Diana S. "From Barbarism to Civilization: Travels of a Latin American Text." *American Literary History* 4, no. 3 (1992): 443–63.

Griffith, Cyril E. *The African Dream: Martin R. Delany and the Emergence of Pan-African Thought.* University Park: Pennsylvania State University Press, 1975.

Gruez, Kisten Silva. *Ambassadors of Culture: The Transamerican Origins of Latino Writing.* Princeton: Princeton University Press, 2002.

Guevara, Gema R. "Inexacting Whiteness: '*Blanqueamiento*' as a Gender-Specific Trope in the Nineteenth Century." *Cuban Studies* 36 (2005): 105–28.

Guterl, Matthew Pratt. "An American Mediterranean: Haiti, Cuba, and the American South." In *Hemispheric American Studies,* edited by Caroline Levander and Robert Levine, 96–115. New Brunswick: Rutgers University Press, 2007.

———. *American Mediterranean: Southern Slaveholders in the Age of Emancipation.* Cambridge: Harvard University Press, 2008.

Hall, Julie E. "Sophia Peabody Hawthorne." In *American Women Prose Writers, 1820–1870,* edited by Amy E. Hudock and Katharine Rodier, 143–51. Farmington Hills: Gale, 2001.

———. "Coming to Europe, Coming to Authorship: Sophia Hawthorne and Her *Notes in England and Italy.*" *Legacy* 19, no. 2 (2002): 137–51.

Hall, Stewart. *Representation: Cultural Representations and Signifying Practices.* 1997. London: SAGE Publications, 2003.

Hames-García, Michael. "Which America is Ours?: Martí's 'Truth' and the Foundations of 'American Literature.'" *Modern Fiction Studies* 49, no. 1 (2003): 19–53.

Hamblen, Abigail A. "Louisa May Alcott and the Racial Question." *University Review* 37 (1971): 307–13.

Havard, John. "Mary Peabody Mann's 'Juanita': Cuba and US National Identity." *Studies in the Novel* 44, no. 2 (2012): 144–63.

———. "Mary Peabody Mann's *Juanita* and Martin R. Delany's *Blake*: Cuba, Urban Slavery, and the Construction of Nation." *College Literature* 43, no. 3 (2016): 509–40.

Hawes, Clement. "Three Times Round the Globe: Gulliver and Colonial Discourse." *Cultural Critique* 18 (1991): 187–214.

Hawthorne, Julian. "Introduction." In *The Story of Evangelina Cisneros (Evangelina Betancourt Cosio y Cisneros), Told by Herself.* New York: Continental Publishing Company, 1898.

Hendler, Glenn. "Civility and Citizenship: Martin Delany's Black Public Sphere." *Public Sentiments: Structures of Feeling in Nineteenth-Century American Literature.* Chapel Hill: University of North Carolina Press, 2001.

———. "The Limits of Sympathy: Louisa May Alcott and the Sentimental Novel." *American Literary History* 3, no. 4 (1991): 685–706.

Hogle, Jerrold E., ed. *The Cambridge Companion to Gothic Fiction.* Cambridge: Cambridge University Press, 2002.

Höglund, Johan. *The American Imperial Gothic: Popular Culture, Empire, Violence.* Farnham, UK: Ashgate, 2014.

Hoveler, Diane Long and Tamar Heller. *Approaches to Teaching Gothic Fiction: The British and American Traditions.* MLA, 2003.

Howe, Julia Ward. *A Trip to Cuba.* Boston: Ticknor and Fields, 1860.

Hughes, William, David Punter, and Andrew Smith, eds. *The Encyclopedia of the Gothic,* Malden: Wiley & Sons, 2016.

Johnson, Sarah. *The Fear of French Negroes: Transcolonial Collaborations in the Revolutionary Americas.* Berkeley: University of California Press, 2012.

Kahn, Robert M. "The Political Ideology of Martin Delany." *Journal of Black Studies* 14, no. 4 (1984): 415–40.

Kaplan, Amy. "Manifest Domesticity." *American Literature* 70, no. 3 (1998): 581–606.

———. *The Anarchy of Empire in the Making of U.S. Culture.* Cambridge: Harvard University Press, 2002.

——— and Donald E. Pease. *Cultures of United States Imperialism.* Durham: Duke University Press, 1993.

Keyser, Elizabeth Lennox. *Whispers in the Dark: The Fiction of Louisa May Alcott.* Knoxville: The University of Tennessee Press, 1993.

Khair, Tabish. *The Gothic, Postcolonialism and Otherness: Ghosts from Elsewhere.* New York: Palgrave Macmillan, 2009.

King, Rosamond S. *Island Bodies: Transgressive Sexualities in the Caribbean Imagination.* Gainesville: University Press of Florida, 2014.

Kirk, John M. "José Martí and the United States: A Further Interpretation." *Journal of Latin American Studies* 9, no. 3 (1977): 275–90.

Kitch, Sally L. *The Specter of Sex: Gendered Foundations of Racial Formation in the United States.* Albany: State University of New York Press, 2009.

Kutzinski, Vera M. *Sugar's Secrets: Race and the Erotics of Cuban Nationalism.* Charlottesville: University of Virginia Press, 1993.

Lasarte Valcárcel, Javier. "Nación por caridad: El mestizaje en *Cecilia Valdés* (y Martí)." *Hispamérica* 35, no. 103 (2006): 17–32.

Lazo, Rodrigo. "Against the Cuba Guide: The 'Cuba Journal,' Juanita and Travel Writing." In *Reinventing the Peabody Sisters,* edited by Monika M. Elbert, Julie E. Hall, and Katharine Rodier, 180–95. Iowa City: University of Iowa Press, 2006.

———. "Filibustering Cuba: *Cecilia Valdés* and a Memory of Nation in the Americas." *American Literature* 74, no. 1 (2002): 1–30.

———. "Historical Latinidades and Archival Encounters." In *The Latino Nineteenth Century,* edited by Rodrigo Lazo and Jesse Alemán, 1–19. New York: New York University Press, 2016.

———. *Writing to Cuba: Filibustering and Cuban Exiles in the United States.* Chapel Hill: The University of North Carolina Press, 2005.

Leary, John Patrick. *A Cultural History of Underdevelopment: Latin America in the U.S. Imagination.* Charlottesville: University of Virginia Press, 2016.

Levander, Caroline. "Confederate Cuba." *American Literature* 78, no. 4 (2006): 821–45.

Levine, Robert S. *Martin Delany, Frederick Douglass, and the Politics of Representative Identity.* Chapel Hill: The University of North Carolina Press, 1997.

Lionnet, Francoise. "Narrating the Americas: Transcolonial *Mettisage* and Maryse Condé's *La migration des coeurs.*" In *Mixing Race, Mixing Culture: Inter-American Literary Dialogues,* edited by Monica Knapp and Debra J. Rosenthal, 65–87. Austin: University of Texas Press, 2002.

———. "Transnationalism, Postcolonialism or Transcolonialism? Reflections on Los Angeles, Geography, and the Uses of Theory." *Emergences* 10, no. 1 (2000): 25–35.

Lomas, Laura. *Translating Empire: José Martí, Migrant Latino Subjects, and American Modernities.* Durham: Duke University Press, 2008.

López Cruz, Humberto. "'Cecilia Valdés': La mulatería como símbolo de identidad nacional en la sociedad colonial cubana." *Hispanófila* 125 (1999): 51–61.

López-Rodríguez, Miriam. "The Short Story as Feminist Forum: Louisa May Alcott's 'Pauline's Passion and Punishment.'" In *Scribbling Women & the Short Story Form: Approaches by American & British Women Writers,* edited by Ellen Burton Harrington, 37–46. Bern: Peter Lang, 2008.

Lowe, John Wharton. *Calypso Magnolia: The Crosscurrents of Caribbean and Southern Literature.* Chapel Hill: The University of North Carolina Press, 2016.

Lowry, Elizabeth. "The Flower of Cuba: Rhetoric, Representation, and Circulation at the Outbreak of the Spanish-American War." *Rhetoric Review* 32, no. 2 (2013): 174–90.

Lugones, Maria. "Heterosexualism and the Colonial/Modern Gender System." *Hypatia* 22, no. 1 (2007): 186–209.

Luis, William. "*Cecilia Valdés:* The Emergence of the Antislavery Novel." *Afro-Hispanic Review* 3, no. 2 (1984): 15–19.

Mann, Mary Peabody. *Juanita: A Romance of Real Life in Cuba Fifty Years Ago.* Edited by Patricia Ard. 1887. Charlottesville: University of Virginia Press, 2000.

Marshall, Megan. *The Peabody Sisters: Three Women Who Ignited American Romanticism.* New York: Mariner Books, 2006.

Martí, José. Carta a Manuel Mercado. *Memorial a José Martí*. http://www.sld.cu/galerias/pdf/sitios/pdvedado/documemtos_imprescindibles_1.pdf

———. "La verdad sobre los Estados Unidos." Biblioteca Virtual Universal, 2010, http://www.biblioteca.org.ar/libros/157587.pdf

———. *Martí on the U.S.A.* Edited and translated by Luis A. Baralt. Carbondale: Southern Illinois University Press, 1966.

———. "Nuestra América." In *José Martí: Nuestra América*, edited by Juan Marinello. Biblioteca Ayacucho, 1985.

———. *Selected Writings*. Edited and translated by Esther Allen. New York: Penguin Books, 2002.

Martin, Robert K. and Eric Savoy. *American Gothic: New Interventions in a National Narrative*. Iowa City: University of Iowa Press, 1998.

McBride, Christopher Mark. *The Colonizer Abroad: American Writers on Foreign Soil, 1846-1912*. New York: Routledge, 2004.

McGann, Jerome, ed. *Blake, or The Huts of America: A Corrected Edition*. Cambridge: Harvard University Press, 2017.

Méndez Rodenas, Adriana. "Tropics of Deceit: Desire and the Double in Cuban Antislavery Narrative." *Cuban Studies* 128 (1999): 83–99.

Mignolo, Walter D. "Introduction: Coloniality of Power and De-Colonial Thinking." In *Globalization and the Decolonial Option*, edited by Walter D. Mignolo and Arturo Escobar. New York: Routledge, 2013.

——— and Michael Ennis. "Coloniality at Large: The Western Hemisphere in the Colonial Horizon of Modernity." *The New Centennial Review* 1, no. 2 (2001): 19–54.

Miller, Floyd J., ed. "Introduction." In *Blake or the Huts of America*, by Martin R. Delany. Boston: Beacon Press, 1970.

Mishra, Vijay. "The Gothic Sublime." In *A New Companion to the Gothic*, edited by David Punter, 288–306. Hoboken: Blackwell Publishing, 2012.

Montero, Oscar. *José Martí: An Introduction*. New York: Palgrave Macmillan, 2004.

Morrison, Karen Y. *Cuba's Racial Crucible: The Sexual Economy of Social Identities, 1750-2000*. Bloomington: Indiana University Press, 2015.

———. "Whitening Revisited: Nineteenth-Century Cuban Counterpoints." In *Africans to Spanish America: Expanding the Diaspora*, edited by Sherwin K. Bryant and Rachel Sarah O'Toole, 163–85. Champaign: University of Illinois Press, 2012.

Morrison, Toni. *Playing in the Dark: Whiteness and the Literary Imagination*. New York: Vintage Books, 1992.

———. *The Origin of Others*. Cambridge: Harvard University Press, 2017.

Moya, Paula M. L., and Ramon Saldívar. "Fictions of the Trans-American Imaginary." *Modern Fiction Studies* 49, no. 1 (2003): 1–18.

Mulcahy, Matthew. *Hurricanes and Society in the British Greater Caribbean, 1624–1783*. Baltimore: The Johns Hopkins University Press, 2008.

Muller, Gilbert H. *William Cullen Bryant: Author of America*. New York: State University of New York Press, 2008.

Mulvey, Laura. "Visual Pleasure and Narrative Cinema." *Visual and Other Pleasures*. New York: Palgrave Macmillan, 2009.

Nwankwo, Ifeoma C. K. "The Promises and Perils of African-American Hemispherism: Latin America in Martin Delany's 'Blake' and Gayl Jones's 'Mosquito.'" *American Literary History* 18, no. 3 (2006): 579–99.

Paraskovich, Jack. *The Wrong View of History*. Bloomington: Xlibris, 2016.

Paravisini-Gebert, Lizabeth. "Colonial and Postcolonial Gothic: The Caribbean." In *The Cambridge Companion to Gothic Fiction*, edited by Jerrold E. Hogle, 229–58. Cambridge: Cambridge University Press, 2002.

Peabody, Sophia. *The Cuba Journal, 1833–1835*. Edited by Claire M. Badaracco. Library of Congress, 1981.

Pérez, Louis A., Jr. *Cuba and the United States: Ties of Singular Intimacy*. Athens: The University of Georgia Press, 1990.

———. *Cuba between Empires 1878–1902*. Pittsburgh: University of Pittsburgh Press, 1983.

———. *Cuba in the American Imagination: Metaphor and the Imperial Ethos*. Chapel Hill: The University of North Carolina Press, 2008.

———. *Cuba under the Platt Amendment*. Pittsburgh: University of Pittsburgh Press, 1986.

———. *Slaves, Sugar, & Colonial Society: Travel Accounts of Cuba, 1801–1899*. Wilmington: Scholarly Resources, Inc., 1992.

———. *The War of 1898: The United States and Cuba in History and Historiography*. Chapel Hill: The University of North Carolina Press, 1998.

Pérez Firmat, Gustavo, ed. *Do the Americas Have a Common Literature?* Durham: Duke University Press, 1990.

———. *The Havana Habit*. New Haven: Yale University Press, 2010.

Peterson, Thomas G. "U.S. Intervention in Cuba, 1898: Interpreting the Spanish-American-Cuban-Filipino War." *OAH Magazine of History* 12, no. 3 (1998): 5–10.

Phillips, Kristine. "Pulitzer Prize-winning author Junot Diaz accused of sexual misconduct, misogynistic behavior." *The Washington Post*. May 6, 2018. https://www.washingtonpost.com/news/arts-and-entertainment/wp/2018/05/05/pulitzer-prize-winning-author-junot-diaz-accused-of-sexual-misconduct-misogynistic-behavior/?noredirect=on&utm_term=.d7ed20d27ebd.

Prados-Torreira, Teresa. *Mambisas: Rebel Women in Nineteenth-Century Cuba*. Gainesville: University Press of Florida, 2005.

Pratt, Mary Louise. *Imperial Eyes: Travel Writing and Transculturation*. New York: Routledge, 1993.

Procter, James, and Angela Smith. "Gothic and Empire." In *The Routledge Companion to Gothic,* edited by Catherine Spooner and Edna McCoy, 95–104. New York: Routledge, 2007.

Punter, David. *A Companion to the Gothic.* Hoboken: Blackwell Publishing, 2000.

——— and Glennis Byron. *The Gothic.* Hoboken: Blackwell Publishing, 2004.

Quijano, Aníbal. "Coloniality and Modernity/Rationality." In *Globalization and the Decolonial Option,* edited by Walter D. Mignolo and Arturo Escobar, 22–32. New York: Routledge, 2010.

——— and Immanuel Wallerstein. "Americanity as a Concept, or the Americas in the Modern World-System." *International Social Science Journal* 44, no. 134 (1992): 549–57.

Raimon, Eve Allegra. *The "Tragic Mulatta" Revisited: Race and Nationalism in Nineteenth-Century Antislavery Fiction.* New Brunswick: Rutgers University Press, 2004.

Rodríguez, María Soledad. "'That mixture of Spain and Alabama': Cuba and Cubans in texts by Louisa May Alcott and Kate Chopin." In *Prospero's Isles: The Presence of the Caribbean in the American Imaginary,* edited by Diane Accaria-Zavala and Rodolfo Popelnik. Oxford: Macmillan Publishers Limited, 2004.

Rosaldo, Renato. "Imperialist Nostalgia." *Representations,* no. 26 (1989): 107–22.

Rosenthal, Debra J. *Race Mixture in Nineteenth-century U.S. and Spanish American Fictions: Gender, Culture, and Nation Building.* Chapel Hill: University of North Carolina Press, 2004.

Rotker, Susana. *The American Chronicles of José Martí: Journalism and Modernity in Spanish America.* Lebanon: University Press of New England, 2000.

Rowe, John Carlos. *Literary Culture and U.S. Imperialism.* New York: Oxford University Press, 2000.

———, ed. *Post-Nationalist American Studies.* Berkeley: University of California Press, 2000.

Sachsman, David B. and David W. Bulla, eds. "Introduction." *Sensationalism: Murder, Mayhem, Mudslinging, Scandals, and Disasters in 19th-Century Reporting.* New York: Transaction Publishers, 2013.

Said, Edward W. *Culture and Imperialism.* New York: Knopf, 1993.

———. *Orientalism.* New York: Penguin Books, 1978.

Saldívar, José David. *The Dialectics of Our America: Genealogy, Cultural Critique, and Literary History.* Durham: Duke University Press, 1991.

———. *Trans-Americanity: Subaltern Modernities, Global Coloniality, and the Cultures of Greater Mexico.* Durham: Duke University Press, 2012.

Saldívar, Ramón. "Comparing Modern Literatures Worldwide: The Transamerican View." *Comparative Literary Studies* 50, no. 2 (2013): 199–203.

Sarmiento, Domingo F. *Facundo: Or, Civilization and Barbarism.* Introduction by Ilan Stavans. Translated by Mary Mann. New York: Penguin Books, 2002.

Savoy, Eric. "The Rise of the American Gothic." In *The Cambridge Companion to Gothic Fiction*, edited by Jerrold E. Hogle, 167–88. Cambridge: Cambridge University Press, 2002.

Schermerhorn, Calvin. *The Business of Slavery and the Rise of American Capitalism, 1815–1860.* New Haven: Yale University Press, 2015.

Scholl, Diane G. "Fallen Angels: Sophia Hawthorne's Cuba Journal as Pièce de Résistance." *Nathaniel Hawthorne Review* 35, no. 1 (2009): 23–45.

Schriber, Mary Suzanne, ed. *Telling Travels: Selected Writings by Nineteenth-Century American Women Abroad.* Dekalb: Northern Illinois University Press, 1995.

———. *Writing Home: American Women Abroad, 1830–1920.* Charlottesville: University of Virginia Press, 1997.

Schulenburg, Chris T. "*Cecilia Valdés*: The Search for Cuban Discursive Control." *Afro-Hispanic Review* 27, no. 2 (2008): 115–32.

Schwarzmann, Georg Michael. "Introduction." *Syncing the Americas: José Martí and the Shaping of National Identity.* Lanham: Bucknell University Press, 2017.

Scott, Rebecca J. *Slave Emancipation in Cuba: The Transition to Free Labor, 1860–1899.* Princeton: Princeton University Press, 1985.

Shanahan, Mark and Stephanie Ebbert. "Junot Díaz case may be a #MeToo turning point." *The Boston Globe.* June 30, 2018. https://www.bostonglobe.com/metro/2018/06/30/junot-diaz-case-may-metoo-turning-point/3TMFseenE4Go1eVsqbFSxM/story.html?s_campaign=breakingnews:news letter.

Siegel, Kristi, ed. *Issues in Travel Writing: Empire, Spectacle, and Displacement.* New York: Peter Lang, 2002.

Sivils, Matthew Wynn. "Gothic Landscapes of the South." In *The Palgrave Handbook of the Southern Gothic*, edited by Susan Castillo Street and Charles Crow, 83–93. London: Palgrave Macmillan, 2016.

Smith, Andrew and William Hughes, eds. *Empire and the Gothic: The Politics of Genre.* New York: Palgrave Macmillan, 2003.

Smith, Harold F. "A Bibliography of American Travellers' Books about Cuba Published before 1900." *The Americas* 22, no. 4 (1966): 404–12.

Smith-Rosenberg, Carroll. *This Violent Empire: The Birth of an American National Identity.* Chapel Hill: University of North Carolina Press, 2010.

Sommer, Doris. "Who Can Tell? Filling in Blanks for Villaverde." *American Literary History* 6, no. 2 (1994): 213–33.

Spangler, Ryan Anthony and Georg Michael Schwarzmann, eds. "Preface." *Syncing the Americas: José Martí and the Shaping of National Identity.* Lanham: Bucknell University Press, 2017.

Spooner, Catherine and Emma McEvoy. *The Routledge Companion to Gothic.* New York: Routledge, 2007.

Stavans, Ilan. "Introduction." In *Facundo, or Civilization and Barbarism*, by Domingo F. Sarmiento. Translated by Mary Mann. New York: Penguin Books, 1998.

Stern, Madeleine B., ed. *Behind a Mask: The Unknown Thrillers of Louisa May Alcott*. New York: William Morrow & Company, 1975.

———, ed. *Critical Essays on Louisa May Alcott*. Boston: G. K. Hall & Company, 1984.

———. *Louisa May Alcott: From Blood and Thunder to Hearth and Home*. Boston: Northeastern University Press, 1998.

———, ed. *Louisa May Alcott Unmasked: Collected Thrillers*. Boston: Northeastern University Press, 1995.

Stoller, Ann Laura, ed. *Haunted by Empire: Geographies of Intimacy in North American History*. Durham: Duke University Press, 2006.

Streeby, Shelley. *American Sensations: Class, Empire, and the Production of Popular Culture*. Berkeley: University of California Press, 2002.

Sugden, Edward. "The Globalisation of the Gothic South." In *The Palgrave Handbook of the Southern Gothic*, edited by Susan Castillo Street and Charles Crow, 69–79. London: Palgrave Macmillan, 2016.

Sundquist, Eric J. *To Wake the Nations: Race in the Making of American Literature*. Cambridge: Harvard University Press, 1993.

Thiong'o, Ngũgĩ wa. *Decolonising the Mind: The Politics of Language in African Literature*. Portsmouth: Heinemann, 1986.

Thomas, Hugh. *Cuba, the Pursuit of Freedom*. New York: Harper & Row, 1971.

Utset, Marial Iglesias. *A Cultural History of Cuba during the U.S. Occupation, 1898–1902*. Translated by Ross Davidson. Wilmington: University of North Carolina Press, 2011.

Valenti, Patricia Dunlavy. *Sophia Peabody Hawthorne: A Life, Vol. 1 1809–1847*. Columbia: University of Missouri Press, 2004.

———. *Sophia Peabody Hawthorne: A Life, Vol. 2, 1848–1871*. Columbia: University of Missouri Press, 2015.

Villaverde, Cirilo. *Cecilia Valdés; or, El Angel Hill: A Novel of Nineteenth-Century Cuba*. Edited by Sibylle Fischer. Translated by Helen Lane. New York: Oxford University Press, 2005.

———. *Cecilia Valdés: Novela de costumbres cubanas*. Edited by Raimundo Lazo. 1882. México, D. F.: Editorial Porrúa, 2006.

Wallerstein, Immanuel. *Geopolitics and Geoculture: Essays on the Changing World-System*. 1991. New York: Cambridge University Press, 1994.

White, Hayden. *Metahistory: The Historical Imagination in Nineteenth-Century Europe*. Baltimore: The Johns Hopkins University Press, 1973.

Wilcox, Carol. "Cuba's 'Hot Little Rebel' and Spain's 'Criminal Fugitive': The Prison Escape of Evangelina Cisneros in 1897." *Sensationalism: Murder, Mayhem, Mudslinging, Scandals and Disasters in 19th-Century Reporting*. New Brunswick: Transaction Publishers, 2013.

Williams, Susan S. *Reclaiming Authorship: Literary Women in America, 1850–1900*. Philadelphia: University of Pennsylvania Press, 2006.

Willis, Nathaniel Parker. *Health Trip to the Tropics*. New York: Scribner, 1854.

Windell, Maria A. "Moor, *Mulata*, Mulatta: Sentimentalism, Racialization, and Benevolent Imperialism in Mary Peabody Mann's *Juanita*." *J19: The Journal of Nineteenth-Century Americanists* 2, no. 2 (2014): 301–29.

Winter, Kari J. *Subjects of Slavery, Agents of Change: Women and Power in Gothic Novels and Slave Narratives, 1790–1865*. Athens: The University of Georgia Press, 1992.

Woertendyke, Gretchen J. *Hemispheric Regionalism: Romance and the Geography of Genre*. New York: Oxford University Press, 2016.

Yang, Sharon Rose and Kathleen Healey, eds. *Gothic Landscapes: Changing Eras, Changing Cultures, Changing Anxieties*. New York: Palgrave Macmillan, 2016.

INDEX

Africanization of Cuba, 97
Ajuria Ibarra, Enrique, 70, 98
Alcott, Bronson, 57
Alcott, Louisa May, 5, 43, 56–58, 57n40, 59n50, 65n56, 86; duality in, 44; Martí and, 127–28. *See also* "Pauline's Passion and Punishment" (Alcott)
Alcott, May, 57
Aldana Reyes, Xavier, 98n12
Alemán, Jesse, 11n34, 13, 14, 18, 139, 149
Alvarez-Amell, Diana, 97–98, 100n20
American exceptionalism, 4, 9, 10, 32, 55, 66
"American Gothic," 13
Americanity, 6n18, 7, 7n20, 8, 10, 11
American Monthly, The, 26
"American Studies," 209n65
annexation, 37–40, 90–91, 117n49, 146

Bannett, Nina, 60n51
Baptist, Edward E., 2

Beidler, Philip D., 9, 15, 95n5, 100n19, 106
Belnap, Jeffrey, 129
Benítez-Rojo, Antonio, 147
Biggio, Rebecca Skidmore, 49–50, 56
"Black Legend," 24, 32–33, 35–37, 39, 41, 90, 112
Blake, of the Huts of America (Delany), 43; duality in, 44, 47, 52–55; publication of, 55–56; slavery in, 50–52, 55–56; transamericanity in, 48–49, 53; white paranoia in, 49–50
Blanco, María del Pilar, 70–71
Blanco, Richard, 1
blanqueamiento, 25n10
Braham, Persephone, 124–25
Braudy, Leo, 145–46
Bray, Katie, 6n17, 14n52
Brickhouse, Anna, 11, 11n32, 24n9, 26, 37, 45, 48, 68
Brooks, Maria Gowen, 25n15
Brown, John, 48

Bryant, William Cullen, 5, 21, 23–27, 25n10, 25n15, 29–31, 33–34, 36–39
Buscaglia-Salgado, José F., 104n24
Byron, Glennis, 145n3, 148

Cap, Piotr, 6n16
Casanova-Vizcaíno, Sandra, 98n12
Castillo Street, Susan, 44–45
Castro, Raúl, 1n1
Castronovo, Russ, 14
Cecilia Valdés (Villaverde), 94–107, 118–19; duality in, 94, 106; gothic emplotment in, 101–4, 106; gothic geoculture in, 97–98; mulatta/o in, 99–100; publishing history of, 93n1; racialization in, 94; slavery and, 99–100, 105; "tragic mulatta" in, 101–5; writing of, 93
Cisneros, Evangelina, 5, 6n15, 11, 94, 110–12. See also *Story of Evangelina Cisneros, Told by Herself, The* (Cisneros)
"Cisneros Affair," 109
Civil War, 4, 43, 47, 80, 90, 109, 137, 139
coartación, 37
Concepción Valdés, Gabriel de la, 53
corruptive gothiscape, 7, 20, 23, 34, 39, 41, 144
Cortina, Rodolfo J., 147n7
Crow, Charles L., 44–45
Cuba: Africanization of, 97; annexation of, 37–40, 90–91, 117n49, 146; Cisneros as, 110–12; of cultural imagination, 9; as gothic double of United States, 52–53; as gothic geoculture, 43, 66, 79, 87, 98; normalization of relations with, 1, 1n1; protagonist role of, 3; as US South, 45–47, 60; as woman in distress, 16, 107–8, 132
"Cuba guide," 23, 40–41
Cuba Journal (Peabody), 83, 89; demonic possession in, 67, 74, 76–77; evolution of, 72–73; Hawthorne and, 68, 73; *Juanita* and, 69;

83; Lazo on, 69; Orientalism in, 76; slavery in, 68–69, 72; transgressive haunting in, 70–71, 78, 91–92. See also Peabody, Sophia
Cuban exiles, 4–5, 5n14, 25, 38, 45

Dana, Richard Henry, Jr., 22, 37, 46
decolonial transamericanity, 7; identity and, 123; in Martí, 123–24, 139–40. See also transamericanity
DeGuzmán, Maria, 32, 34n32, 107
DeLaMotte, Eugenia, 144
Delany, Martin R., 5, 43, 46, 48n20, 53n32, 54n32. See also *Blake, of the Huts of America* (Delany)
demonic possession, 65–67, 74, 76–77
Díaz, Junot, 143–45, 143n1
Doolen, Andy, 49
doubles. See duality
Douglass, Frederick, 47
duality: in Alcott, 44, 47, 58–59, 61–62; in Delany, 44, 47, 52–55; in *Juanita*, 80–83; in Villaverde, 94, 101, 106
Duncan, Cynthia, 99n15

Edwards, Justin D., 15, 24, 98, 112n47, 148
Elbert, Monika, 13
Elbert, Sarah, 57
Eljaiek-Rodríguez, Gabriel, 145–46
Emerson, Ralph Waldo, 127
Eve, 72, 75
exceptionalism, 10, 55, 141
exiled Cubans, 4–5, 5n14

factuality, 95–96, 112
Facundo: Or, Civilization and Barbarism (Sarmiento), 130–31
Fall of Man, 72
fear, 5–6, 6n16, 53, 122–24, 132–33
Fern, Fanny, 26
Fernández, Raúl, 129
Fischer, Sybille, 104

Foner, Philip S., 5n13, 126–27
Forza, Daniela Ciani, 78
Fountain, Anne, 141

García Márquez, Gabriel, 147, 147n8, 149
garrote, 29, 36
Gelpí, Juan, 103, 105
gender, 7, 14n46, 16, 29, 40, 47, 59, 59n50, 61–63, 96n7, 103–4, 107, 112, 132–34. *See also* women
genderized race, 29
geoculture, 7–8, 7n19, 44, 99–100, 103, 105, 118, 138, 143–44. *See also* gothic geoculture
Gillman, Susan, 13
Gilroy, Paul, 134, 134n25
Glissant, Eduardo, 8n22
Goddu, Teresa A., 13
Goodrich, Diana S., 131n23
gothic emplotment, 7, 93–119; factuality and, 95–96; racialization and, 95; in Villaverde, 101–4, 106
gothic geoculture, 144; Cuba as, 43, 66, 79, 87, 98; defined, 6; in *Juanita*, 87; in Villaverde, 97–98
Gothic South, 45
gothicized souths, 7, 18, 43, 48, 49, 53, 56, 66
gothiscape, 23–25, 23n4, 33–34, 39–41, 69, 144
Guardini Vasconcelos, Sandra, 15, 24, 98, 148
Guevara, Gema R., 102n22
Gulliver's Travels (Swift), 36
Guterl, Matthew Pratt, 12, 12n38, 12n40, 44

Haitian Revolution, 2, 97
Hames-García, Michael, 137, 141
Harpers Ferry, 48
Havana Habit, The (Pérez Firmat), 1–2
"Havana habit," 3

Havard, John, 53n32, 79–81, 80n39, 87, 90–91
Hawai'i, 117n49
Hawthorne, Julian, 94, 108–13
Hawthorne, Nathaniel, 67–69, 73, 78
Health Trip to the Tropics (Willis), 22
Healy, Kathleen, 23
Hearst, William Randolph, 108–9
Hendler, Glenn, 52n28
Heredia, José María, 4, 25, 25n15
Höglund, Johan, 13
Hospital Sketches (Alcott), 128
Howe, Julia Ward, 22, 46, 108
Hughes, William, 22n2
"Hurricane, The" (Heredia), 25

Illustrated Newspaper, 59
imperialism, 5–6, 15, 32n29, 45, 87, 106, 124, 133
Incidents in the Life of Slave Girl (Jacobs), 26
intersectionality, 29

Jackson, Helen Hunt, 128
Jacobs, Harriet, 26
Johnson, Sarah E., 126–27
journalism, yellow, 108–9
Juanita (Mann), 53n32, 68, 79–80; annexation and, 90–91; *Cuba Journal* and, 69–70, 83; duality in, 80–83; racialization in, 86–87; slavery in, 70–71, 81–82, 84–86; "tragic mulatta" trope in, 86–88; transgressive haunting in, 70–71, 91–92. *See also* Mann, Mary Peabody

Kahn, Robert M., 47–48
King, Rosamond, S., 40
Kitch, Sally L., 29
Kutzinski, Vera M., 97

Lasarte Varcárcel, Javier, 105n29

168 • INDEX

Lazo, Rodrigo, 3–4, 5n14, 17, 23, 32, 40, 45, 69, 99–100, 105, 118, 149
Leary, John Patrick, 9–10, 16n57, 94n3, 138, 146–47
Leslie, Frank, 59
Letters of a Traveler: Notes of Things Seen in Europe and America (Bryant), 21
Levander, Caroline, 8
Lionnet, Françoise, 126n8
Little Women (Alcott), 56–57
Lomas, Laura, 140
Longfellow, Henry Wadsworth, 127
López, Narciso, 93n2
López Cruz, Humberto, 97, 99n16
López-Rodríguez, Miriam, 58–59, 65
Lowry, Elizabeth, 108, 117
Lucifer, 72
Lugones, Maria, 14n46
Luis, William, 93n2, 99

madness, 23n4, 50–51, 67, 74
Maine, U. S. S., 109
male gaze, 27n22
Manifest Destiny, 32n29
Mann, Horace, 80
Mann, Mary Peabody, 5, 53n32, 68–70, 130
manumission, 37
Marshall, Bridget M., 13
Martí, José, 4–5, 11, 121–22, 125–28, 126n8, 147n7; fear in, 124, 132–33; identity in, 123, 130; monster in, 124–25, 128–29, 134–40; racialization in, 135. *See also* "Our America" (Martí); "Truth about the United States, The" (Martí)
McBride, Christopher Mark, 46
McGann, Jerome, 48n20, 54, 56
McKinley, William, 109, 117n49
Mercado, Manuel, 122
Mignolo, Walter, 7–8, 7n19, 8n22, 124, 148–49

Miller, Floyd J., 48
Milton, John, 72
Mishra, Vijay, 23n4
monster, 6, 19, 44, 47, 98, 112, 117, 122–25, 128–29, 134–40, 145–46
Montero, Oscar, 128
Moods (Alcott), 57n40, 65n56
Morrison, Karen Y., 17n63, 25n10
Morrison, Toni, 13, 145
Moya, Paula M. L., 8
Mulvey, Laura, 27n22

"Negroes in Cuba.—Indian Slaves" (Bryant), 29
New Americanists, 20n65
New York Evening Post, 25
New York Journal, 94, 109, 116. *See also Story of Evangelina Cisneros, Told by Herself, The* (Cisneros)
New York Mirror, 26
newspapers, 108–9
normalization of relations, 1, 1n1
North Star (newspaper), 47
Notes in England and Italy (Peabody), 73, 73n23
Nwankwo, Ifeoma C. K., 48

Obama, Barack, 1, 1n1
Orientalism, 74, 76, 112
Origin of Others, The (Morrison), 145
Ortiz, Inés, 98n12
O'Sullivan, John L., 32n29, 141
Other, 28, 32, 116, 130, 144–45, 149
"Our America" (Martí), 125, 128–34, 140

Pan-Africanism, 48
Paradise Lost (Milton), 72
"Pauline's Passion and Punishment" (Alcott), 43; duality in, 44, 47, 58–59, 61–62; publishing of, 59; racialization in, 59–62; womanhood in, 61

Peabody, Sophia, 5, 59n50, 83, 88n48, 131n23. See also *Cuba Journal* (Peabody)
Pérez, Louis A. Jr., 15–16, 22–23, 106–7, 107n34, 108n40, 112
Pérez Firmat, Gustavo, 1–4, 9
Philippines, 117n49
Platt Amendment, 117n49
Poe, Edgar Allan, 26
"poetics of haunting," 71
postcolonial gothic, 145n3
Prados-Torreira, Teresa, 6n15, 94
Pratt, Mary Louise, 24, 29, 40
Puerto Rico, 5, 117n49
Punter, David, 145n3

Quijano, Aníbal, 6n18, 7, 7n20, 10n29, 14n46, 124
Quiroga, Juan Facundo, 130

racialization: in Alcott, 59–62; in Cisneros, 94, 110–11; gothic emplotment and, 95; in *Juanita*, 86–87; in Mann, 86–87; in Martí, 135; in Villaverde, 94
racialized gaze, 35
racialized gender, 29, 87
Raimon, Eve Allegra, 102
Ramona (Jackson), 128
"Rappaccini's Daughter" (Hawthorne), 78
Rodríguez, Maria Soledad, 65n56
romance genre, 96, 96n7, 117–18
Rosaldo, Renato, 40n41
Rosenthal, Debra J, 62n53
Rostenberg, Leona, 56
Rotker, Susana, 130
Ruth Hall (Fern), 26

Said, Edward, 141n38
Saint-Domingue, 2, 45
Saldívar, José David, 11, 139–40
Saldívar, Ramón, 8, 10n29, 11

Sarmiento, Domingo F., 130
Schermerhorn, Calvin, 2
Scholl, Diane, 72
Schwarzmann, Georg Michael, 126n8, 128n18
sensationalism, 108–9
Silva Gruez, Kirsten, 9n24, 10–11, 25, 25n15
slavery: Alcott and, 57–58; and American South, 46–47; in American writing, 22–23; in Bryant, 36–39; in *Cuba Journal*, 68–72; in Delany, 49–52, 55–56; as geoculture, 7–8, 44, 99–100, 103, 105, 118, 138, 143; in *Juanita*, 70–71, 81–82, 84–86; in Mann, 79–83, 85–86, 90–91; in Morrison, 145; Other and, 145, 144; in Peabody, 70–71; transamericanity and, 44; in Villaverde, 99–100; women and, 29, 50
Slaves, Sugar, & Colonial Society: Travel Accounts of Cuba, 1801–1899 (Pérez), 22
Smith, Andrew, 22n2
South: American, 44–47, 60, 135–36; Cuba as, 45–46; Gothic, 45
Spain, 32–33, 34n32, 93n2, 107–8
Spangler, Ryan Anthony, 126n8, 128n18
Spanish-American War, 5, 5n13, 107, 109
Stavans, Ilan, 131n23
Stern, Madeleine, 56, 58
Story of Evangelina Cisneros, Told by Herself, The (Cisneros), 107–19; factuality in, 112; and Hawthorne, Julian, 108–12; Hearst and, 108–9; introduction to, 109–13; racialization in, 94, 110–11; sensationalism and, 108–9; Spain in, 107–8
"Story of the Island of Cuba, A" (Bryant), 25–26
Stowe, Harriet Beecher, 49
Sugden, Edward, 45
Sundquist, Eric J., 52, 55
Swift, Jonathan, 36

Thoreau, Henry, 57n40
"tragic mulatta," 86–88, 101–5
transamericanity, 12–13, 15, 23–25, 40, 44, 48–49, 53, 59, 66, 70, 71, 76, 85, 95, 99, 100, 107, 112, 119, 123–25, 129, 134, 141, 144, 148. See also decolonial transamericanity
transcendentalism, 79
transcoloniality, 126, 134
transgressive hauntings, 7, 70–71, 78, 91–92
Trip to Cuba, A (Howe), 22
"tropical Gothic," 15
tropics, as term, 12
Trump, Donald, 1n1
"Truth about the United States, The" (Martí), 121, 125, 134–41
tuberculosis, 3
Turner, Nat, 48, 57

Uncle Tom's Cabin (Stowe), 49
United States: Civil War, 4, 43, 47, 80, 90, 109, 137, 139; Cuba as gothic double of, 52–53; exceptionalism of, 10, 55, 141; in Martí, 136–37; as monster, 138–39; South, 44–47, 60, 135–36
U. S. S. *Maine*, 109

Vacation Voyage, A (Dana), 22

Valenti, Patricia Dunlavy, 68, 73–75, 89n49
Villaverde, Cirilo, 4–5, 11, 32n29, 93, 93n2. See also *Cecilia Valdés* (Villaverde)

Wallerstein, Immanuel, 6n18, 7, 7n19–7n20, 10n29, 18n64
Warwick, Adam, 57n40
White, Hayden, 96, 96n7
"white paranoia," 49–50
whiteness, 25n10, 111
Whitman, Walt, 127
Wilcox, Carol, 109, 119
Williams, Susan S., 45–46
Willis, Nathaniel Parker, 5, 21–24, 25n10, 26–29, 31–32, 34–36, 39–40
Willis, Sara Payson, 26
Windell, Maria, 91
Winter, Kari J., 117n50
Woertendyke, Gretchen J., 45
women, 16, 26–30, 27n22, 34–35, 40, 50–52, 107. See also gender; "tragic mulatta"

Yang, Sharon Rose, 23
"yellow journalism," 108–9

Zayas, Fernando, 75

GLOBAL LATIN/O AMERICAS
FREDERICK LUIS ALDAMA AND LOURDES TORRES, SERIES EDITORS

This series focuses on the Latino experience in its totality as set within a global dimension. The series will showcase the variety and vitality of the presence and significant influence of Latinos in the shaping of the culture, history, politics and policies, and language of the Americas—and beyond. We welcome scholarship regarding the arts, literature, philosophy, popular culture, history, politics, law, history, and language studies, among others. Books in the series will draw from scholars from around the world.

Gothic Geoculture: Nineteenth-Century Representations of Cuba in the Transamerican Imaginary
    IVONNE M. GARCÍA

Affective Intellectuals and the Space of Catastrophe in the Americas
    JUDITH SIERRA-RIVERA

Spanish Perspectives on Chicano Literature: Literary and Cultural Essays
    EDITED BY JESÚS ROSALES AND VANESSA FONSECA

Sponsored Migration: The State and Puerto Rican Postwar Migration to the United States
    EDGARDO MELÉNDEZ

La Verdad: An International Dialogue on Hip Hop Latinidades
    EDITED BY MELISSA CASTILLO-GARSOW AND JASON NICHOLS

www.ingramcontent.com/pod-product-compliance
Lightning Source LLC
Chambersburg PA
CBHW020949230426
43666CB00005B/233